INTERCULTURAL CITIZENSHIP IN THE POST-MULTICULTURAL ERA

SAGE SWIFTS

In 1976 SAGE published a series of short 'university papers', which led to the publication of the QASS series (or the 'little green books' as they became known to researchers). More than 40 years since the release of the first 'little green book', SAGE is delighted to offer a new series of swift, short and topical pieces in the ever-growing digital environment.

SAGE *Swifts* offer authors a new channel for academic research with the freedom to deliver work outside the conventional length of journal articles. The series aims to give authors speedy access to academic audiences through digital-first publication, space to explore ideas thoroughly, yet at a length which can be readily digested, and the quality stamp and reassurance of peer review.

INTERCULTURAL CITIZENSHIP IN THE POST-MULTICULTURAL ERA

RICARD ZAPATA-BARRERO

Los Angeles | London | New Delhi
Singapore | Washington DC | Melbourne

Los Angeles | London | New Delhi
Singapore | Washington DC | Melbourne

SAGE Publications Ltd
1 Oliver's Yard
55 City Road
London EC1Y 1SP

SAGE Publications Inc.
2455 Teller Road
Thousand Oaks, California 91320

SAGE Publications India Pvt Ltd
B 1/I 1 Mohan Cooperative Industrial Area
Mathura Road
New Delhi 110 044

SAGE Publications Asia-Pacific Pte Ltd
3 Church Street
#10-04 Samsung Hub
Singapore 049483

Editor: John Nightingale
Assistant editor: Eve Williams
Production editor: Martin Fox
Copyeditor: Mary Dalton
Proofreader: Leigh C. Smithson
Marketing manager: Susheel Gokarakonda
Cover design: Wendy Scott
Typeset by: C&M Digitals (P) Ltd, Chennai, India
Printed in the UK

© Ricard Zapata-Barrero 2019

First published 2019

Apart from any fair dealing for the purposes of research or private study, or criticism or review, as permitted under the Copyright, Designs and Patents Act, 1988, this publication may be reproduced, stored or transmitted in any form, or by any means, only with the prior permission in writing of the publishers, or in the case of reprographic reproduction, in accordance with the terms of licences issued by the Copyright Licensing Agency. Enquiries concerning reproduction outside those terms should be sent to the publishers.

Library of Congress Control Number: 2019938908

British Library Cataloguing in Publication data

A catalogue record for this book is available from the British Library

ISBN 978-1-5264-7705-7
WEB PDF 978-1-5264-9849-6

At SAGE we take sustainability seriously. Most of our products are printed in the UK using responsibly sourced papers and boards. When we print overseas we ensure sustainable papers are used as measured by the PREPS grading system. We undertake an annual audit to monitor our sustainability.

To Isabel and Samjhana, for their presence and understanding

CONTENTS

Introduction: Citizenship and diversity nexus revisted – the intercultural citizenship focus   x

PART I POST-MULTICULTURAL CONTEXT AND THE NEED OF A PRAGMATIC TURN IN DIVERSITY POLICY DEBATES   1

1 The policy narrative context of diversity dynamics today   3

Introduction: Setting the debate on the intercultural citizenship paradigm   3
1. Continuities and changes in the post-M era: Revisiting boundless multiculturalism   6
2. The place of intercultural citizenship in the post-M framework debate and beyond   12
3. The intercultural citizenship acquit: The pragmatic turn and its consequences   15

2 Avenues of origin of intercultural citizenship: The European local turn in diversity policies   19

Introduction: The seminal focus and the geography of the intercultural citizenship paradigm   19
1. The multi-faceted European avenues of intercultural citizenship: An emerging policy debate during the European Year of Intercultural Dialogue   21
2. The decisive task of the Council of Europe in providing a distinctive European meaning to intercultural citizenship: The city framework   23

3. The urban face of intercultural citizenship: Shaping
   micro-politics and a policy of proximity   26
4. Origins and first premises of the intercultural policy
   narrative in scholarly debates   28

3 Intercultural turn in Europe: In a diverse Europe, what does 'Europeanness' mean today?   32

Introduction: The European Union's governance of migration-related
   diversity – an on-going project   32
1. EU ontological crisis: In search of a We-European, which
   includes migration-related diversity   33
2. Migrants as pioneers of Europe? How migrants can help
   to reboot European identity   36
3. Can the EU survive without a sense of EU Community? The EU as
   machinery generating frustrated second-generation migrants   39
4. Final remarks: Interculturalism, a distinctive value of
   European identity   41

4 The business card of intercultural citizenship: Distinctive features   46

Introduction: Intercultural citizenship in times of
   diverse complexity   46
1. Methodological interculturalism: Breaking down
   epistemological barriers   49
2. Intercultural citizenship and mainstreaming policies:
   Elective affinity   51
3. Transnational citizenship and intercultural citizenship:
   Overlapping affinities   53
4. New horizons: Cosmopolitanism and solidarity   57

PART II FOUNDATIONS OF INTERCULTURAL CITIZENSHIP   61

5 Conceptualizing intercultural citizenship's diversity-linkage theory   63

Introduction: Contact theory, the basis of intercultural citizenship   63
1. Relational sociologists' contributions on the variety of contacts   66
2. Intercultural citizenship as a strategy of building relationships   69
3. Summary: Intercultural citizenship's people linkage theory   73

6 Normative policy drivers of intercultural citizenship: a comprehensive view   76

Introduction: Guiding questions to discuss normative drivers of intercultural citizenship   76
1. Three hypotheses on diversity – without intervention   77
2. Zooming in on the three normative policy drivers of intercultural citizenship   79
3. Intercultural citizenship: A comprehensive approach   86

7 Republicanism, public space and intercultural citizenship   87

Introduction: The context of intercultural citizenship's practice – public spaces   87
1. The place of public spaces within the three traditions of citizenship: the republican view of intercultural citizenship   90
2. Republicanism provides to intercultural citizenship a reflection of urban spatiality and place-making   92
3. Public spaces' social assets: People-to-place linkages in diversity settings   94
4. Conditions for the use of intercultural public spaces   97

8 The social benefits of intercultural citizenship: Diversity as a public good   100

Introduction: Diversity as a public good   100
1. Intercultural citizenship as a mediator for linking diversity and advantages: An overview   102
2. Antiracism, against xenophobia and interculturalism   106
3. Well-being, quality of life, cohesion, human rights and democracy   108

Concluding roadmap: Summarizing what the reader has found in this book   112

References   117
Index   135

INTRODUCTION: CITIZENSHIP AND DIVERSITY NEXUS REVISTED – THE INTERCULTURAL CITIZENSHIP FOCUS

In the globalized and interconnected world, the movement of people between countries is becoming the norm. All societies consist – and have always consisted – of a web of diverse influences, interactions and exchanges, a situation that is becoming more complex as globalization takes hold. The increasingly diverse population (of cultures, nationalities, languages, religions, etc.) that stands in our cities is then a direct consequence of human mobility that brings with it globalization. While a strong growth process throws up new challenges for converging countries, there is ample evidence that public policies can make a difference. Public institutions, in whatever level of government, have become aware that diversity cannot be left alone. They then assume that this diversification must be managed, because without intervention it tends to generate political isolation, social division, territorial segregation, daily xenophobia and racism, and even ideological extremism. The key question that frames these public debates is often focused on how to live together, stressing the sociological dimension that diversity creates. I would suggest also underlining the political dimension, which stresses the need of governments to find appropriate tools and approaches to manage diversity. Following Schuck (2006: 6–7), I will describe diversity management as 'how government self-consciously approaches diversity', so long as one bears in mind that 'manage' includes both decisions to make diversity a subject of political and legal intervention and decisions to leave diversity to informal, unregulated choices.

In other words, the premise of this book, regarding diversity governance, is that there is no other way to govern it than through social engineering. Diversity is a mainstream dynamic of liberal democratic societies, and to formulate arguments against diversity is as unrealistic as to be against globalization.

This belongs to our historical course of action, and what is needed is to discuss how to govern it in order that it does not contradict the basic democratic liberal values of human rights, equality, fundamental freedoms, and social values of solidarity, cohesion and stability; the reason being that 'dynamics' means that diversity has a transformative effect into social and political spheres, and involves increasing complexity and multiple identities. These differentiation categories may explain discriminatory and unequal, precarious and unbalanced power situations. Policies and politics may also react and/or influence these dynamics through narratives and collective actions engaging stakeholders and other public/private networks of actors.

While this policy awareness is key to recognizing the unavoidability of diversity dynamics in our societies, the problem remains that this diversity-recognition still faces many difficulties to be fully permeated within the social and political structures – although, and most importantly, it meets many difficulties in attempting to penetrate the same people's mindsets.

The debate about how to govern diversity, how to live together, will be done following a citizenship focus. This is not surprising. The diversity/citizenship nexus has three main features following the three main dimensions of citizenship. On the one hand, the liberal dimension of citizenship tells us that it is a way to focus the debate around what is seen as the main challenge liberal democracies must face today: the spread of the principle of equality of rights for all in the new particular settings of complex diversity and in the framework of human rights. That is, whatever category of diversity differentiates people (be it cultural, race, religion, nationality), they must all have the same treatment and opportunities. On the other hand, the communitarian dimension focuses on citizenship as a community-building process, in the sense that it is through citizenship that we channel the need to ensure a common public identity, and keep a minimum sense of belonging, into a society that is characterized by being diverse. This membership dimension of citizenship is also completed with the republican dimension, which puts emphasis on participation, civic duties and common practices in the public realm, a shared public culture. Equal Rights, community-building and public practice are then the three main drivers that will feature the citizenship focus.

This citizenship focus will be combined with the diversity category. As a direct product of global human movement, the concept of diversity that I will use will be directly related to the differences migrants bring to us and thus make us aware of our taken-for-granted lifestyles and worldviews. Even if we do not adhere to the mainstream religion of Christianity, we celebrate Christmas and Easter, and most of our festivities have a religious background. This mirror effect that the diversity dynamics provokes is what falls within the diversity category, but also when these differences become social and political categories, basically cultural, ethnic, racial, national, religious beliefs and even language differences. Of course, this is not an argument to deny the pertinence of having an expansive view of diversity (Vertovec, 2015: 2), which also includes other categories of social difference such as gender, social class, sexual orientation, physical ability, mental ability, age, education, etc. This involves an incorporation of the analysis of diversity as an intersectional-based approach, or what has been popularized as super-diversity (Vertovec, 2007). For instance, considering that inequalities and discriminations never have one root-cause but are always the combination of several interlinked categories of diversity. From this perspective there is an obvious vital link between diversity and citizenship, in the sense that the social differentiations that are produced become the main factors of discrimination and inequality of rights, disperse the sense of belonging to the same community, and can desegregate the public realm and sphere of civic behaviour and participation. In some way the categories of analysis of diversity and citizenship help us to keep the critical focus we would like to follow, and it is our particular way of generating awareness.

Let me also introduce some caveats about the central concept of interculturalism. At its root, interculturalism means 'cultural exchange'. So, it is by definition a relational concept. It has become a category of practice rather than a category of analysis following the differences put forward by Brubaker (2012). It emphasizes the fact that two agents exchange their culture (in a broad sense, as worldview) through contact. From a policy point of view, interculturalism is a range of different kinds of policies developed in the name of contact promotion and knowledge exchange. Interculturalism is becoming a new orthodoxy of diversity management, a new guiding policy for diversity engineers. As such it is only recently that it has penetrated into the scholarly debate, from city planners and other different avenues we will see later. Its narrative had to be placed close enough to interculturalism and far away, at the beginning as a contrast and now as complementary to multiculturalism, filling most of its gaps. Behind this policy narrative there is a sense of equality, power-sharing, democracy and human rights, less a sense of justice that has governed the multicultural narrative, but it also has a normative dimension since it seeks to produce social benefits as a result of its implementation. These results can even be viewed as public goods: cohesion, solidarity, well-being, creativity, etc. The focus on citizenship will from the very beginning enable us to clarify that interculturalism is, beyond whatever other consideration, a public philosophy that allows for a learning and socializing process for people living in new diverse environments, and what I will call a culture of diversity.

At this crossroads on diversity studies, migration studies and citizenship studies, I will place the focus of this book. In defending intercultural citizenship I am enhancing the importance of including all the people living in a diverse society, independently of their legal status (national citizens, citizens with migrant origin, non-citizens), since I take into consideration that national citizens have been completely set aside in migration-related diversity debates during the dominance of the multicultural narrative, with the dramatic consequence that they have easily adhered to the view that 'diversity is the other', placing it in the basket of conflict, instability and social separation. This neglect, together with a lack of emphasis on inter-personal contact, and the difficulties of embracing new complex patterns of diversity, has today nurtured the 'disenchantment' of the multicultural citizenship narrative.

The debate on intercultural citizenship will be placed from the very beginning within the mainstream discussion on multicultural citizenship and national-civic citizenship, as different ways of understanding the place of diversity in our societies, its effects, and consequently the different ways to govern it. These two approaches of linking citizenship and diversity also do not manage to see that many of the problems arising from diverse societies are due to a lack of contact and mutual knowledge. This is the basis of the intercultural citizenship approach. The premise of this philosophical ideology is to think of diversity on its own terms, and not from state-homogeneous parameters that tend to interpret it in security and instability terms, as an alteration of a national tradition. Living together in diversity cannot be anything other than the product of learning and the result of socialization that public authorities should be responsible for providing to the entire population. We need to recognize that the former multicultural citizenship approach completely neglected the claims of national citizens, which are also in need of new parameters to live within diversity contexts. And the first thing that must be achieved is that the population recognizes diversity and becomes aware of its irreversibility. Soon we will all be 'others'! Without this prerequisite, people will hardly have the predisposition to make positive contact with others, but will always be negatively oriented by prejudices and stereotypes. Furthermore, this diversity-recognition can act as an antidote against any kind of fundamentalism (be it supremacist or Islamist) that may want to impose its own worldview on others.

We also know that in some ways the intercultural citizenship debate is not new. It already exists as an internal debate within at least two main disciplines. In the education debate there is an emphasis on the importance of developing intercultural skills and competencies as a learning process of citizenship in schools. It has also been used to focus on an international dimension of citizenship: in this case as an opportunity to engage in international dialogue, thus reducing the prejudices engendered by national perspectives (Byram, 2011). It is the way, from my view, that Kymlicka (2003) dealt for the first time with intercultural citizenship in an unusual article, where he demonstrated the difficulty in understanding intercultural citizenship beyond the cross-state international relations approach.

The rationale behind this book has been structured in two main parts. **Part I** is contextual and it moves from diagnosis and descriptions (Chapters 1–2) to looking ahead to theoretical reflections and propositions (Chapters 3–4). Chapter 1 sets the debate on the intercultural citizenship paradigm within the post-multicultural (post-M) era, and Chapter 2 portrays the different avenues of its origin, with the purpose of framing the distinctive features of the European view, basically based on cities. Then in Chapter 3 I will review the ontological crisis of Europe today and propose that interculturalism could be a way to reboot European identity and the European citizenship debate. I will close this Part with Chapter 4, presenting what I will call the 'business card of intercultural citizenship', stressing first the epistemological assumptions behind methodological interculturalism, and then arguing how intercultural citizenship can be clustered into the consolidated patterns of mainstream policies, transnationalism, cosmopolitanism and solidarity, all of which today dominate the migration-related diversity agenda.

Part II will enter into the foundations of intercultural citizenship. I will again follow four chapters. The first two chapters will set up the descriptive and normative dimensions of intercultural citizenship, respectively. Chapter 5 will draw roughly on the diversity-linkage theory, which sustains most of the intercultural conceptual building. Chapter 6 will go to the normative drivers giving meaning to intercultural citizenship. Chapter 7 will discuss another foundational feature of intercultural citizenship: the particular view of public space and the way intercultural citizenship is close to the republican citizenship tradition. Finally, Chapter 8 will close this Part with a brief overview of empirical studies that focus on the benefits of diversity and may sustain intercultural citizenship. The essay will end by drawing a concluding roadmap summarizing what the reader has found in this book.

* * * * *

Author's note: This book collects the arguments I have been putting forward during recent years, engaged in the recent debate on Multiculturalism and Interculturalism, and channelling my ideas through the focus of citizenship. I consider this book as being the culmination of these last thinking-in-process years on interculturalism. I would like to express my acknowledgements to Carmen Ruiz (English reader), Iren Eylül Karaoglu Tunç (Proof reader) and Karina Melkonian (Indexer).

PART I

POST-MULTICULTURAL CONTEXT AND THE NEED OF A PRAGMATIC TURN IN DIVERSITY POLICY DEBATES

I

THE POLICY NARRATIVE CONTEXT OF DIVERSITY DYNAMICS TODAY

INTRODUCTION: SETTING THE DEBATE ON THE INTERCULTURAL CITIZENSHIP PARADIGM

Diversity management is lacking reference points after a backlash against multiculturalism (Vertovec and Wessendorf, 2010) and the increasing support for xenophobic political parties, most of which are also Eurosceptic (Chopin, 2015). The financial crisis has also forced many European governments and administrations to cut back on budgets originally destined for immigration policies. Most of them are even claiming they must produce policies at zero cost (Scholten et al., 2016), withdrawing or diverting initial specific policies regarding mainstreaming policies. This, together with the associated increases in competition for resources between host and migrant communities, is reducing solidarity (Kymlicka, 2016a). The new context of superdiversity (Vertovec, 2007) and the fact that multiple identities and transnational practices are becoming the norm are evidence that we are entering a post-ethnic period where factors such as birth-origin and nationality do not necessarily drive diversity policies; other factors such as social class, gender, age, current legal situation and working conditions also come into play. The fact that the securitization framework has penetrated most diversity-management thinking, preventing more open, cosmopolitan and humanistic policies towards newcomers and those who have already been living in reception societies for some time, and the fact that in recent years strong trends have emerged showing that second-generation migrants are embracing radical outlooks, are signs of a very extreme situation for the core project of multicultural Europe (Modood et al., 2006). Brexit and the end of free movement for European Union (EU) workers also poses serious difficulties in maintaining one of the markers of European identity, namely, European citizenship (Zapata-Barrero, 2016a), and it certainly contributes to the need to reframe the European project. In such times of turmoil and in this context of a crisis of ideas, intercultural citizenship may help light the way, enjoying as it does some traction in policy and political spheres, and some support from experts and in academic circles, indispensable conditions for being considered a policy paradigm (Hall, 1993; Hogan and Howlett, 2015).

Seen through a European lens, the current process by which the re-nationalization of policies, xenophobia, racism and intolerance are becoming a new 'political ideology' is framing public opinion and political discourses, and legitimizing policies (Triandafyllidou et al., 2011; Zapata-Barrero and Triandafyllidou, 2012). Scholarly work highlights that while this originates in cultural anxiety, it also emerges from approaches to welfare chauvinism, entrenched inequalities and emerging insecurity, all of which are also nurtured by the inconsistencies arising from the management of diversity and complex issues such as access to European territory.

Populism and neo-conservatism are the main forms that this new ideology takes. Most of the public debate around migration and diversity is essentially focused either on the explanatory level, seeking to identify the main factors provoking such an emergence, or on the strategies seeking to invade political power and governments, but much less so on the political and policy instruments we have for preventing and reducing the conditions that make it possible. It is here where the intercultural citizenship paradigm can play a prominent role.

The pressing situation today is clear: the loss of support for multiculturalism has dragged a lack of support for diversity management in the current post-multicultural (post-M) atmosphere. The latest European Commission against Racism and Intolerance (ECRI) report, for instance, signals a growing anti-immigrant sentiment and Islamophobia as being among the key trends in 2015 (ECRI, 2016). The recent Islamist terrorist attacks in Paris, Copenhagen, Nice, Berlin and Barcelona further add to the Islamophobic sentiment being misused by populist political parties to stir up prejudice and hatred against Muslims in general. Likewise, the decision taken in June 2016 by the UK to leave the European Union (Brexit) is also connected to anti-immigrant sentiments. The supremacists' attacks in America, Europe and Oceania are also negative waves of this against-diversity ideology. Key questions arise today that cannot be answered with former policy paradigms: Can the multicultural citizenship paradigm counter the extremist and/or the re-nationalist narratives? Can the multicultural citizenship paradigm today be a marker of European identity without creating more political cleavages at the national level?

This scenario illustrates that we cannot understand the emergence of the intercultural citizenship paradigm from a static perspective. It must be seen as being the result of a historical process and a multi-factorial outcome that today reframes the migration-related diversity policy debate. The best way to focus this discussion is in terms of continuities and changes, and to approach it in terms of policy paradigm change and formation (Zapata-Barrero, 2017d).

In this context, intercultural citizenship fundamentally proposes a change of focus in managing diversity: the policy lens moves from a static, centrepoint approach (based on an individual or group agent) to a much more dynamic and network approach, one that results from interpersonal contact and multiple diversity-based relations. Interculturalists agree on the backlash of multiculturalism literature (Vertovec and Wessendorf, 2010), which has been charged with causing self-segregation and with engendering more inequality and separation among people of different cultures. This 'multicultural question', however, is not new. From the beginning, the link between multiculturalism and equality has been disputed, in terms of the social consequences of policies recognizing cultural differences. The most seminal normative argumentation still remains Barry's (2001) egalitarian criticism of the politics of multiculturalism. We can also quote Hall (2000: 235), who aptly summarizes:

> How then can the particular and the universal, the claims of both difference and equality, be recognised? This is the dilemma, the conundrum – the multicultural question – at the heart of the multicultural's transruptive and reconfigurative impact.

The normative discussion of the multicultural literature always attempts to rectify the consequences of increasing marginalization that emerge from social and political structures. It focuses on the principle of equality, understood as redistribution of wealth and recognition of cultural rights (Frazer and Honneth, 2003). Surely, within this criticism of social egalitarianism, the Cantle report (2001) stands as one of the great efforts in dealing with conflictive empirical evidence, at a time when the UK suggested that it was the lack of social cohesion that led to northern city tensions in 2001, paving the way for less multicultural policies, while increasing uneasiness regarding the supposed segregation of minority communities.

As an approach to diversity management, intercultural citizenship also seeks to break the congealed view of identity and belonging. It endorses this detachment from any attempt to align culture with genetics, as though it were hereditary like skin colour (Bloomfield and Bianchini, 2001: 104). We can also include here Phillips' (2007) *Multiculturalism without Culture* argument, in which she claims that it is time to elaborate a version of multiculturalism that dispenses with reified notions of culture, in favour of a version that engages more ruthlessly with cultural stereotypes.

Individual preferences and practices, rather than national origin adscriptions, prevail as a policy framework. Let me give an example: to be of Moroccan origin does not entail being Muslim and following Islamic beliefs. It would be the same if I refused to be ascribed as Christian in Morocco, but was nonetheless subjected to certain multicultural policies because of this institutional pre-categorization. In a nutshell, what interculturalists claim is that we must let people decide their cultural practices, their religions and their languages, independent of the national circumstances into which they were born. Interculturalism is about first asking how people recognize their identities, and it then respects their self-identification. This also includes a respect for the diversity of identities within the same national-cultural category. I am thinking, for instance, that even if Morocco does not officially recognize cultural diversity among their own nationals (for instance, Amazigh or Berber culture), multiculturalism contributes to this homogenization of Moroccan culture by being too nationality-dependent in ascribing the cultural identities of people of Moroccan origin.

The main purpose of this first chapter is to place intercultural citizenship within this diversity debate. I will follow three main lines of argumentation. First, I will review the continuities and changes of the multicultural narrative. This will allow me, second, to place the debate within the present-day process of a post-M period. The role played by the emerging national civic citizenship paradigm (a renovated version of assimilation), prioritizing duties before rights, is also considered crucial to better contextualize intercultural citizenship. Third, and as a consequence, I will try to elucidate what the main policy implications are, namely that intercultural citizenship notifies a pragmatic turn in diversity debates.

1. CONTINUITIES AND CHANGES IN THE POST-M ERA: REVISITING BOUNDLESS MULTICULTURALISM

The multicultural citizenship paradigm has dominated recent decades, holding a monopoly over the narrative on how to reconcile Unity and Diversity, and essentially following the equality and human rights principles on diversity management, with a normative conception of justice in the background. We know that there are different perspectives of how each scholar focuses on diversity, equality and human rights interface (Crowder, 2013; Laden and Owen, 2007; Mansouri and Ebanda de B'beri, 2014; Triandafyllidou et al., 2011; Wise and Velayutham, 2009). To summarize multicultural citizenship's nuclear core, its main project is the inclusion of immigrants in the mainstream by respecting their differences and recognizing their distinctive cultural practices, religions and languages. Economic distribution and political participation are also two of the main building blocks (Kymlicka, 2010). Recently some scholars have focused on the multicultural citizenship paradigm in terms of indicators rather than principles (Banting and Kymlicka, 2013; Bloemraad and Wright, 2014; Levy, 2000; 125–60; Murphy, 2012; and even Vertovec, 2010), providing additional specific evidence-based structural and legal arrangements to ensure the non-alienation of specific groups. In such empirical studies multiculturalism has deployed most of its tools for the protection of rights, for the containment of exceptional cases within the mainstream public policy system, and legitimating specific policies basically in terms of funding, recognition and affirmative action. And a certain group-based approach has been dominant in the application of the principles, without incorporating a more critical view of what kind of cultures deserve recognition and under what terms.

Sharing this evidence-based approach, and fully aware that times have changed, Kymlicka highlights some contextual factors that today challenge the multicultural citizenship paradigm. He illustrates, for instance, that:

> existing theories of liberal multiculturalism presuppose, implicitly or explicitly, that state-minority relations are 'desecuritized' – that is, the governance of state-minority relations is seen as an issue of social policy to be addressed through the normal democratic process of claims-making, consultation, and debate, not as an issue of state security that trumps normal democratic processes. (2015: 241)

He also signals that some of the conditions of multiculturalism are eroding:

> Liberal multiculturalism, I would argue, was theorized for situations in which immigrants were seen as legally authorized, permanently settled, and presumptively loyal. In an age of securitization and super-diversity, these assumptions are put into question. Early theories of multiculturalism now seem at best incomplete, and at worst out-dated, resting on assumptions and preconditions that may no longer apply. (2015: 244)

As Kymlicka (2010) foresaw, the new historical phase that we are presently in is characterized by the fact that most of the multicultural criticism comes not from a far-right, anti-immigrant and nationalist discourse, but from inside multiculturalism. I consider myself within this trend. What Kymlicka was claiming is the need to reframe multiculturalism within a new context, something we can label, for want of a better term, as the 'post-M era'. It is within this new phase that I would like to place the current emergence of the intercultural citizenship paradigm.

I am aware that the term 'post-M' could contribute to confusion rather than clarification if conceptually it is not well defined (Bradley, 2013; Gozdecka et al., 2014; Ley, 2005). Primarily it involves a need to merge the Unity/Diversity dimensions that have featured throughout the diversity policy debates of recent decades, incorporating the contextual factors framing the new times of turmoil that were described herein at the outset. This basically means that today, where a plurality of identities and transnational minds has become the norm, where diversity is seeking to enter mainstream policies, to argue about how to deal with diversity-related socio-economic and power relations in terms of we-unity and them-diversity is to condemn the new reality to distortion, fuelling the arguments of its detractors. It also implies that we are in a process of policy paradigm change, where most of the main pillars of the multicultural citizenship paradigm remain, but with a rising awareness that the acceptance of differences following the equality principle cannot be defended without requiring a justification. And legitimate proof cannot come from liberal and democratic principles (the initial project of multicultural citizenship) alone, but need to be formulated essentially in terms of a new common public culture, a culture of diversity, as I will defend through these pages.

Also belonging to this trend is the growing conviction that in settings of complex diversity, tolerance needs to be limited (Dobbernack and Modood, 2013; Zapata-Barrero and Triandafyllidou, 2012). This debate certainly comes in a context where the multicultural citizenship paradigm is at one of its lowest moments (Lewis, 2014), under suspicion of having promoted segregation rather than union, of giving rise to ethnic conflicts rather than a common culture, of struggling to offer grounds for community cohesion and social capital (Cantle, 2008), and even of legitimating affirmative actions. Today, there is a growing awareness that multicultural policies have fuelled far-right xenophobic political parties. In Germany in October 2010 and in the UK in February 2011, political leaders also promoted this argument of state multicultural failure, a backlash against – or even the 'death' of – the multicultural paradigm, provoking deep public discussion across Europe (*Daily Mail Reporter*, 2011).

This growing concern in Europe over the rise of populist anti-immigrant parties and anti-Islamification narratives cannot be disconnected from the disenchantment with multiculturalism. What is new today is the electoral support that some of these political parties have gained in some countries, significantly providing real alternatives for power, and provoking a *contagion effect* to mainstream political parties. The recent general elections in most of the European countries also demonstrated that these parties, after an initial period of conquest, seem to have established themselves in the mainstream political system, and have even reached political power. This has even meant that governments have changed their courses of action, incorporating anti-immigration measures into their strategies for managing diversity (Yılmaz, 2012), a situation that has been aggravated by contradictions within the immigration politics of the liberal states forced by these contextual restraints (Hampshire, 2013). What is specific to the debate on growing radicalism against diversity is that it uses most of the basic normative premises that legitimate the multicultural citizenship paradigm, and in this sense, it is a scholarly forum that must be taken seriously by strong defenders of liberal democratic principles and human rights. It would be lacking in historical insight and academically irresponsible to misinterpret the elite discourses that have framed most of the public debate in Europe in recent years. The 'muscular' defence of liberal democratic principles, to borrow the words of former British Prime Minister Cameron, has provoked an array of criticisms; however, there is a clear purpose for addressing the multicultural question in terms of limits:

> Under the doctrine of state multiculturalism, we have encouraged different cultures to live separate lives, apart from each other and apart from the mainstream. We've failed to provide a vision of society to which they feel they want to belong. We've even tolerated these segregated communities behaving in ways that run completely counter to our values. (Cameron, 5 February 2011)

This means that immigrants must, at minimum, acquire the language of the host country, and learn about its history, norms and institutions. And it entails the introduction of written citizenship tests and loyalty oaths. Implicitly if not explicitly, civic integration is presented as the only tool to limit what we may call a *boundless multiculturalism*.

The backlash against multiculturalism does not express a problem with culture, but rather with its excess, including in its most extreme form the recognition of illiberal values and a lack of human rights' protection. For instance, Banting and Kymlicka (2006: 54) already warned that 'it is very difficult to get public support for multicultural policies if the groups that are the main beneficiaries of these policies are perceived to be carriers of illiberal cultural practices'. Of course, this zero-sum way of seeing multiculturalism and its limits, as it was first articulated by, among others, Joppke (2004, 2008), has to be relativized. The new context is such that, as Vertovec (2010: 92) has notably stressed, 'No politician wants to be associated with the M-word'. To be post-M then does not mean being anti-M, but rather incorporating within the multicultural project the awareness that not everything coming from other cultures can be accepted without a critical mindset.

The national civic turn belongs to this post-M era.[1] Why does this post-M framework emphasize the view of considering national identity as a friend rather than a foe? Because there is a certain shared view that the multicultural citizenship paradigm has exaggerated the rights-based approach to the detriment of duties. And these duties must also be placed at the same level of policy consideration, because they can help to regulate the excessive recognition of certain cultures, and limit illiberal practices contravening human rights. In practical terms, the duties-based approach calls for development of the means to ensure civic practices and citizenship as well as a minimum level of competence in the national language and a minimum level of knowledge about the country's history and society. In normative terms, it seeks to ensure a minimum threshold for living together in a common (national) public culture. It is true that this civic turn can have many readings, depending on how one sets this minimum threshold and whether one makes it voluntary or compulsory. In European terms, taking care not to erode Unity by being 'too diverse', to use Goodhart's (2004) terms, means reevaluating national identity, language and democratic liberal values as limiters of multiculturalism. There is, however, in this new civic-national narrative a problem, which was already visible in the multicultural approach: they both still consider diversity as 'the other' that is separated from the mainstream, instead of placing diversity *within* the mainstream. The question today is no longer how to live *with* diversity but how to live *in* diversity (Antonsich, 2016: 470). The growing diversity scenarios compounding our societies today are new for everybody, whether their origins are Filipino, Pakistani, Moroccan, Chinese, Ecuadorian, French, German, Hungarian or Catalan. There is a general desire to build an alternative to the extremist narrative, and neither the multicultural citizenship paradigm nor the national-civic

---

[1] See Bauböck and Joppke (2010); Goodman (2012); Joppke (2004, 2007); Meer et al. (2015); Mouritsen (2008, 2013).

citizenship paradigm narratives dominating this post-M period provide us with enough convincing arguments that bridge Unity and Diversity. I would even say that this post-M period places multiculturalism under suspicion of being part of the problem needing to be dealt with.

This post-M era also means we are entering a post-racial and a post-ethnic period, as those who oppose multiculturalism see it as having been imposed by racial and ethnic minorities whose demands for recognition were prioritized over all other concerns. The unease surrounding multiculturalism, which has led governments across Europe not only to ban hijabs and burkas but also to install citizenship testing and promote 'national values' (Lentin, 2014: 1272), has less to do with multicultural policies and more to do with fragmentation and the loss of a common public culture. It is a kind of fusing of the Unity and Diversity agendas, or, as King described, post-M as a wide acknowledgement of group distinctions combined with a state struggle to ensure that government policies do not accentuate hierarchical divisions between groups based on race, ethnicity and national background; a struggle rich in historical connotations that can no longer presume a teleological narrative towards the melting pot that is individualism (King, 2005: 122). This claim that Unity also needs to be respected and recognized within Diversity is gaining support from a number of scholars. In terms of rights and duties, this post-M period seeks to focus the debate on the best way to reach some sort of Rawlsian reflective equilibrium, where duties limit the rights-based calls for the recognition of differences.

In this epistemological context, the added value of this post-M framework is not only that it officializes the need to limit the former *boundless multiculturalism* narrative through more civic-national values, but that intercultural citizenship becomes a kind of mediator between the two, placing emphasis on the communicative aspect within Diversity, which also belongs to Unity. This 'civic zeitgeist' describes a set of practices including integration contracts, classes, citizenship tests and ceremonies, acquisition of the language of the host country, and learning about its history, norms and institutions (Meer et al., 2015). This national-civic citizenship paradigm may be said to have the mythical Janus face, since it cannot be interpreted only as part of a more or less hidden nationalistic assimilation agenda, but must also be seen as a policy narrative ensuring equal opportunities and a minimum cultural capital for the development of social capacities in the host society. It can also be seen as an instrument to facilitate a sense of mutual belonging, contact and interaction. This is why the debate cannot dismiss the most radical approach of the civic turn, which fundamentally places duties as a condition for allocating rights. This argument exists in many policymakers' and politicians' minds, and in its radical form (that is 'no rights without duties') it attracts not only right-wing and populist anti-immigrant political parties, but also social-democrat political parties who see that these policy narratives, together with the 'welfare chauvinism' narratives, may help win over more of their electorate.

2. THE PLACE OF INTERCULTURAL CITIZENSHIP IN THE POST-M FRAMEWORK DEBATE AND BEYOND

To my knowledge, the multicultural citizenship paradigm narrative has never formulated a critical interpretative framework regarding the way culturally homogeneous states categorize diversity dynamics. The intercultural argument is that we cannot impose the majoritarian understanding of diversity categories upon others. Ethnicity is self-ascribed, flexible and cannot be imposed by those with the power to define diversity categories. The intercultural citizenship paradigm narrative reacts against the ethnicization of people. This substantial distance from the multicultural citizenship paradigm in the domain of ethnicity, nationalism and race is likewise a departure from what Brubaker calls 'groupism', in other words, 'the tendency to treat ethnic groups, nations and races as substantial entities to which interests and agency can be attributed' (2002: 164). The summary of these arguments is clear. For the most part, the multiple identity reality in which most people live today tells us that birthplace and/or nationality do not determine public identities. To ask someone where he/she was born with the purpose of gaining an initial idea of what public identity he/she holds is not as self-evident as it was in the past. Several studies demonstrate that people's growing mobility is currently pluralizing identities and the self-national and cultural adscriptions (Favell, 2014). This is now the rule, one which needs to be incorporated into the current diversity debate.

The intercultural citizenship paradigm starts out with a claim for greater encounters, considering this to be something lacking in the two former paradigms. In addition to the rights-based and the duties-based approaches, there is a need to focus on contact between people from different backgrounds, including nationals. Interculturalism does not seek ranking as the best way to deal with the accommodation of diversity, but rather to emphasize the need to focus on something that other approaches seem to have taken for granted and that does not automatically occur if there is no specific policy to target it. This contacts-based approach is seen as an integration policy (Guidikova, 2015) and consequently it also needs to be considered as an important driver for a socialization process, of culture-learning and culture-making (Sarmento, 2014: 615). Through contacts, people can acquire what civic integration claims to achieve – knowledge and mutual understanding – and what multicultural integration also seeks to obtain – the combating of diversity-related discrimination and inequalities. It also provides people from different backgrounds, including national citizens, the same opportunities in society. Intercultural citizenship is therefore essentially viewed as an anti-racist tool.[2] This anti-discrimination promotion is a fundamental element since it focuses on the factors that hinder contact zones. There are contextual, legal, institutional and structural factors that reduce people's motivation to interact and even build walls of separation between them based on misinterpretations of differences. Here we take into account legal frameworks concerning voting rights for foreigners and naturalization policies, as well as socio-economic opportunity gaps among citizens, where differences become the factor behind reduced contact. Anti-discrimination promotion also includes tackling disadvantage, as it is hard to see how the intercultural citizenship paradigm can continue over time if one or more sectors of society are so unequal that people are led to believe they have no real stake in that society.

We can say the intercultural citizenship paradigm is a technique for bridging differences and creating bonds and social capital. That is, it promotes relations between people who share certain characteristics (bonds), as well as relations between individuals from different backgrounds (promoting interaction between people across different religions, languages, etc.) who are predisposed to respecting others' differences (Gruescu and Menne 2010: 10). It is a way, then, to avoid the confinement and segregation of people which may condemn them to live in a state of permanent social exclusion.

Most of the premises for legitimacy supporting the intercultural citizenship narrative come precisely in the added value of these relational practices. But we cannot perceive interculturalism as something that should be compulsory, as if it were a perfectionist philosophy. If people do not want to relate, we cannot force them to. The problem arises when we notice that, most of the time, people are not in contact because there are certain constraints that take the form of prejudgements and stereotypes. It is here that many programmes aimed at combating rumours, prejudices and negative perceptions towards diversity are expanding throughout Europe (Council of Europe, 2014). Consequently, we must be aware that while contact is fundamental to

---

[2] The anti-racist dimension of interculturalism has been examined in depth by Gundara (2000, 2005). Only recently has it also been applied in policy studies (Carr, 2016; Pinxten and Cornelis, 2002; Barn, 2012).

intercultural citizenship, it also needs to be supplemented by a positive narrative at the societal level to support the beneficial impact (political leaders' narratives, the media, schools, etc.).

At this point, this policy takes an instrumental form, focusing on the conditions for contact, and it is here that interculturalism meets the multicultural and civic citizenship paradigms. For instance, Meer and Modood (2012) argue that to allow communication, there are certain equality and power-sharing requirements, or, as Levrau and Loobuyck (2013: 622) highlight, the fact that the national-civic citizenship assumes the need for a minimum level of shared language and public culture, setting the basis for communication (see also Barrett, 2013). Intercultural citizenship begins, then, when multicultural and national-civic citizenship policies have developed all their potential; it is not meant to replace them, nor to go against them or before them. Without a certain degree of recognition of rights and fulfilment of duties, contacts can become difficult.

In the age of populism, to use Kymlicka's words (2016b), multicultural master narratives nurture anti-immigrant arguments and feelings, or even radical views of national-civic integration, ranking duties as a condition *sine qua non* of rights. The contacts-based approach of the intercultural citizenship paradigm can thus be seen as an opportunity to break this vicious circle, by bridging the tension between the multicultural citizenship and the national-civic citizenship paradigms. This position of an arbiter must be taken seriously, since it can help to reorient the focus of both policy paradigms. We can perfectly consider that both the multicultural citizenship and the national-civic citizenship paradigms are diversity policy strategies to ensure the necessary conditions for contact. Multiculturalism's concern about equality and power sharing, and the civic-nationalistic concern about minimum standards of language and knowledge on tradition and values, are ultimately contributing to the promotion of 'contact zones'. But the contacts-based approach is not consubstantial with the other two policy paradigms. The intercultural citizenship paradigm cannot be successful if a minimum (but limited) range of multicultural and national-civic conditions are not met. But the fact that multicultural citizenship and national-civic citizenship paradigms are able to create the conditions for contact does not necessarily mean that it will happen. Consequently, there is a need for a policy whose main target is to encourage, and ensure the conditions and opportunities are available for, contact among people. It is here that we can find interculturalism's main scope for legitimization. The golden rule of intercultural citizenship is that through contact people share spaces, socialize in diversity and develop feelings of membership.

There cannot be integration and inclusion without contact between people of different backgrounds. It is through contact that people develop trust and solidarity; it is through contact that people develop a new public culture, a 'culture of diversity'.

This leads us to argue that interculturalism also calls for reassessment of what we may call the 'immigrant/citizenship divide', which has dominated the diversity debate in migration studies. What is interesting here is that the consequence of this divide, which always reproduces a certain discourse where national citizens considered as the 'we' are not the subjects of diversity policies. The multicultural citizenship paradigm (and more explicitly the national-civic citizenship paradigm) has always taken for granted that 'diversity is the others'. In the policy-making process, there is a division of the population between citizens and non-citizens, nationals and non-nationals, immigrants and citizens. This analytical cleavage has the effect of reproducing a certain power relation between majority-national citizens and minority-ethnic citizens or immigrants, a relation that fails to create bridges between these two sets of people. Instead, this framework reinforces the idea of separate categories of people, just as diversity policies have been mainly directed towards one part of the population, be they called immigrants, non-nationals, ethnic minorities, or a range of other conceptualizations in different countries and contexts. Today, in a super-diversity context, in a scenario where second and third generations of migrants live in Europe, where the only attachment to their society of origin comes from their parents (e.g. Crul et al., 2012), most of these so-called citizens have an immigrant background, and consequently this division of the population that probably made sense in earlier stages of the migration process is now very difficult to sustain. This assumption therefore needs to be revised. This follows that we need a more pragmatic approach to deal with diversity governance, without being dominated by rude categorizations.

3. THE INTERCULTURAL CITIZENSHIP ACQUIT: THE PRAGMATIC TURN AND ITS CONSEQUENCES

Intercultural citizenship is the most pragmatic answer to concrete concerns related to diversity management. It highlights that it is a proximate policy, always performance-oriented, with the aim of inverting diversity's initial, potentially negative impact. This direct problem-solving approach is in the very nature of intercultural citizenship.

By virtue of its origins, intercultural citizenship can be seen as a pragmatic policy rebellion of *cities* against the state domination of diversity policies in recent decades. Cities are now organizing welcoming events for newcomers as a way to provide knowledge about the host society and the city, and they also offer language courses as part of the city's public assistance. In contrast, even if multicultural citizenship policies are also developed at the city level, they are always done under an administrative decentralization process beginning at the state level.

This pragmatism is clear-sighted in its origins from expertise knowledge rather than strictly academic. Here we can say that the research/policy nexus debate can help us distinguish the contacts-based policy approach (interculturalism) from the rights-based (multiculturalism) and the duties-based (national-civic) approaches to diversity accommodation. The multicultural citizenship paradigm comes from academia and therefore it has an intellectual origin; it is a product of the 'laboratory', albeit without too much testing at the beginning, and is deontic, universalist and rationalist. It is close to what Scholten (2011) labels an 'enlightenment model' within the research/policy nexus, where academic arguments predominate over policy arguments.

The intercultural citizenship paradigm is an evidence-based policy and, in Scholten's terms, is much closer to an 'engineering model' where the primacy is in the policy, which informs academic arguments. This origin provides the intercultural citizenship paradigm with two main strengths: *proximity*, as it primarily promotes face-to-face relations and develops most of its policies at the micro-level (Zapata-Barrero, 2015a: 187), and *pragmatism*, because action and practice prevail over any preconception of ideal justice or equality 'to the extent that less emphasis is placed on form and culture, and more on the subject that acts and therefore interacts' (Abdallah-Pretceille, 2006: 480).

'Proximity' harks back to three interrelated meanings: (a) *spatiotemporal meaning*: 'proximity' means 'closeness' and, as such, it involves combining time and space. Intercultural citizenship promotes 'face-to-face' interactions, as has been stressed from the beginning. These exchanges and contacts can be found in neighbourhood relationships and in everyday public spaces, such as children's playgrounds, markets, public parks and neighbourhood group events; (b) *political and social meaning*: 'proximity' means 'connectedness', namely that the policy is relevant to citizens. Interculturalism offers concrete responses to citizens' direct challenges. As a policy, it gives immediate response to citizens' daily concerns; (c) *ethical meaning*: 'proximity' means 'empathy', which involves developing values that promote exchange and contact, and generate a sense of, let me say, common humanity. Interculturalism encourages mutual respect and positive social values, promoting socialization and a public culture built on mutual trust, confidence and social capital.

The intercultural citizenship paradigm's primary concerns are not about abstract or universal notions of justice or rights and goods in the context of diversity, as may be the case with multicultural citizenship, but about a society that takes advantage of the resource that diversity offers while also ensuring community cohesion. This 'social ecological background to diversity' is totally absent in both the multicultural citizenship and the national-civic citizenship paradigms.

There are several direct consequences of this pragmatism that belongs now to the intercultural *acquis*. First, this policy paradigm is sustainable, both economically and in terms of human resources (Zapata-Barrero, 2015a). This basically means that the possibility of implementation is much more a matter of political will and technical motivation (and imagination), than one of human and financial resources. If there is a common guiding thread to the edited volume of Scholten and Van Breugel (2017), it is the pattern of relevance that the financial crisis has forced many governments and administrations to cut the budget originally destined for immigration policies, and forced them to produce immigration policies at zero cost. That mainstreaming is in part a consequence of this context of austerity, a pattern to be considered in the next section.

Second, one anchor point is its non-ideological character, in the sense that the city does not take sides towards a particular ideology from the right–left spectrum. The fact is that interculturalism attracts many types of governments and political parties. This means that when it is incorporated as a city agenda for managing diversity, it 'resists' ideological variations in political governments. The international network of Intercultural Cities fostered by the Council of Europe has shown not only that it is politically colour-blind, but also that it is 'resistant' to city-government political changes.[3] These features certainly explain its political attraction and territorial expansion in Europe.

So, even if it is a newcomer in the debates over citizenship and diversity, the intercultural citizenship approach has shown a power of seduction for policy makers, who basically understand that this approach does not force them to target explicit groups, since they interpret affirmative action as being one of the factors of negative public opinion, the rise of xenophobia and anti-immigrant discourses (Zapata-Barrero, 2011). This 'attraction' is then connected with its differentiated policy implications in contrast to multicultural citizenship. From the point of view of governance, intercultural citizenship has even reached a

---

[3]Most intercultural cities have passed the test of elections and changing leadership, as Guidikova (2015) and Zapata-Barrero (2016b) have indicated, among others.

level of consensus between society and politics that did not occur in most cities with other paradigms. This agreement in policy strategy on what, for many years, had been a matter of social dispute and political cleavage, is perhaps the basic argument that supports the need to better articulate this intercultural expansion. The question of 'how to focus diversity policy' becomes more easily accepted politically, then, when the answer is intercultural citizenship. To my knowledge, the multicultural citizenship narrative has not shown such policy-oriented attractiveness at the city level in such a relatively short time. There is empirical evidence that we are seeing an interculturalist wave, but we cannot say that we observe the same wave pattern for multiculturalism in cities. Now, however, it most likely needs to offer distinctive arguments, not necessarily built against other approaches.

Seen from another angle to reach the same conclusion, it is a fact that interculturalism has more elements of political continuity than multiculturalism, which is not widely accepted by the whole political spectrum, and its continuity over time in cities is not fully guaranteed when a change of government occurs. Multicultural citizenship policies have always had a certain problem in being accepted within the realm of public opinion, even before such policies have been put into action (Crepaz, 2006), and intercultural citizenship seems to be more resistant to negative public opinion (Ludwineck, 2015). There is also the technical and administrative argument in justifying that we are beginning a policy-paradigm formation. Intercultural citizenship does not generate immediate social negative effects (such as segregation or separation) that can disturb policy-making plans in the medium or long term (Zapata-Barrero, 2017a). It is also a recognized feature in the emerging intercultural literature that one of its limits is that it has a certain, let us say, 'relative conservative' character, in the sense that it does not favour radical structural changes that may affect the regular patterns of institutional action on policy. The emerging intercultural citizenship policy paradigm does not favour specific structures in society; rather it focuses on diversity policies based on what is common among people with several diversity-categories, rather than differences. This overall feature, which favours some sort of reflective equilibrium between majorities and minorities, paraphrasing Bouchard (2015: 58), is sometimes presented with the mainstreaming metaphor of a policy lens, a wave with expanding purposes all over the basic structures of society. As we have continuously insisted from the very beginning, the only premise required for diving into this policy paradigm is the recognition that the dynamics of diversity are an irreversible fact.

2

AVENUES OF ORIGIN OF INTERCULTURAL CITIZENSHIP: THE EUROPEAN LOCAL TURN IN DIVERSITY POLICIES

INTRODUCTION: THE SEMINAL FOCUS AND THE GEOGRAPHY OF THE INTERCULTURAL CITIZENSHIP PARADIGM

As a policy strategy, intercultural citizenship has its origin in conflict-resolutions. It is then seen as a tool to reach shared views and responsibilities when relations between at least two parts have distant or irreconcilable views. The final purpose is to reach peace and stability. As such, interculturalism is one of the main international relations narratives, basically applied at the global level and within an assumed 'civilizational' framework; and at the regional level, in ethno-religious territorial conflicts. It is through this conflict-based approach that interculturalism penetrated migration and diversity studies only recently. This is the context in which we place the intercultural citizenship paradigm. Our first task, then, is to try to unpin this conflict-based origin, still present in most institutions and policies claiming interculturalism.

In most of the geographical origins of intercultural citizenship this seminal conflict-based approach persists. For instance, it frames most diversity debates in Latin-American countries (Solano-Campos, 2013, 2016; Tubino and Sinnigen, 2013), where it is even recognized constitutionally (Mexico). Interculturalism is seen as a strategy to deal with conflicts related to indigenous people. This view takes shape within the particular theoretical framework linking indigenous tradition and modernity. This debate has been ongoing in Quebec (Bouchard, 2015; Ganon and Iacovino, 2016) and throughout

Canada (Lashta et al., 2016), as well as Australia (Mansouri and Lobo, 2011) since the 1990s and even earlier (Delafenetre, 1997). In this last case, interculturalism forced the political authorities to recognize the territories of the first aboriginal populations. Interculturalism is also used for inter-faith conflict resolutions in territorial ethnic areas such as Lebanon (Yazbeck Haddad and Fischbach, 2015). So, we cannot say that the intercultural policy paradigm is new. Certainly, what probably is new is its application to migration-related issues. In fact, the policy paradigm first entered into migration-related diversity contexts in Quebec, and then in Europe, but with rather different approaches, as I will sketch.

The origins of the intercultural policy narrative stem, like those of the multicultural policy paradigm, from Canada. It developed as a 1980s reaction to the Canadian multicultural policy announced in the 1970s, which placed Québécois identity in the same basket of diversity as the indigenous population and immigrants (the three basic dimensions, which inspired Kymlicka's (1995) view of multiculturalism) and was basically seen as detrimental to the survival of the French language. It claimed that the interrelation between the minority-diverse population and the majority-national (Québécois culture) must be at the centre of the negotiation, and then directly placed the dialogue between Unity and Diversity as the main framework to legitimize policies towards immigrants. This intercultural approach was seen, however, in the context of *multiple diversity*,[1] that is, where two dynamics of diversity interact (the national demands of Quebec and the cultural demands of immigrants), and this policy was considered as an instrument to ensure the survival of the Québécois national identity. Many scholars have articulated this policy philosophy (Gagnon and Iacovino, 2016; Labelle and Rocher, 2009), but the one who without doubt has been the most influential is Bouchard (2015), also largely responsible for the Bouchard-Taylor report (Bouchard and Taylor, 2008), the result of a scholarly and public open debate that laid the foundations of this intercultural philosophy. This vertical view of contact between Unity and Diversity, understood in terms of a power relation between the majority and minorities, constitutes the 'Québécois' view of interculturalism and develops a new contract theory, putting emphasis on some sort of reflective equilibrium between the rights of migrants and their duty to respect the Québécois culture and language (Zapata-Barrero, 2015b). It is true that this application cannot

---

[1] On the concept of multiple diversity, applied in the case of Spain, see Zapata-Barrero (2013).

be understood if we do not contextualize this understanding within a context that the same Québécois describe as a divided society between Anglophone and Francophone communities. Migrant populations are seen as a factor that can change the balance of power, and therefore as one of the most powerful drivers of uncertainty within the Québécois/Canadian conundrum. In fact, there is a widespread recognition that the last referendum for independence (October 1995) was lost in part because the Québécois population of migrant origin voted to remain in Canada. One of the main arguments for losing the independence referendum put forward in the internal Québécois debate was confounded by the difficulties the Québécois political parties had in defining the 'we' and 'citizenship' (Labelle and Salée, 2001; Sklar, 1999) during their campaign.

In my view it is certainly unwise to try to decontextualize this Québécois view of interculturalism by moving this debate to Europe in terms of majority and minority communicative trends, as Modood (2016) has, in my opinion, wrongly recently proposed. We are looking at two contexts, with two different uses of intercultural policy. That said, I am not defending that the Québécois view of interculturalism has no place in Europe, since it can be meaningful, but it is not through this Québécois' view that interculturalism has penetrated Europe. Let us now go to the European context.

The following structure will be followed: in section 1 I will concentrate on how interculturalism basically penetrated Europe during the European Year of Intercultural Dialogue (2008). In the next section I will focus on the Council of Europe and how it has made an effort to foster a distinctive meaning for Europe. Then in section 3 I will draw the local dimension of intercultural citizenship in Europe, and finally I will end with section 4, in which I will review the scholarly debate that has also contributed to its expansion.

1. THE MULTI-FACETED EUROPEAN AVENUES OF INTERCULTURAL CITIZENSHIP: AN EMERGING POLICY DEBATE DURING THE EUROPEAN YEAR OF INTERCULTURAL DIALOGUE

Until recently, interculturalism in Europe was absent in the policy realm. It only started being widely discussed 10 years ago, when the EU declared the Year of Intercultural Dialogue in 2008 and incorporated interculturalism into its agenda. If we read carefully the founding document of the European Year of Intercultural Dialogue (EYID, 2008) we are surprised there is not just one, but three different meanings: (i) as a cross-state strategy to foster better understanding between Member States to support greater cooperation within a social market economy with common values; (ii) as a cross-regional strategy to enable the EU to make its voice better heard in the world and to forge effective partnerships with countries in its neighbourhood, thus extending a zone of stability, democracy and common prosperity beyond the EU, and thereby increasing the well-being and security of European citizens and all those living in the EU; and finally (iii) intercultural dialogue (ICD) has been understood as cultural exchange among people within the EU, leaving open that this cross-people relation can be interpreted both among EU citizens and among people from different cultures or the so-called third-country nationals. The first interpretation has driven most of the mechanisms to promote European identity by fostering relations among EU citizens. But surprisingly, the second view has practically not been widely articulated (we will deal with this issue in Chapter 3).

Following these lines, the Council of Europe's White Paper on Intercultural Dialogue summarizes these three strands when it states that ICD is

> an open and respectful exchange of views between individuals, groups, with different ethnic, cultural, religious and linguistic backgrounds and heritage on the basis of mutual understanding and respect. It operates at all levels – within societies, between the societies of Europe and between Europe and the wider world. (Council of Europe, 2008: 10–11)

This geographical understanding of ICD still remains today. The disembarkation of interculturalism into Europe was contextually justified as part of the EU's response to the combined effects of the successive enlargements, the increased mobility resulting from the single market, old and new migratory flows, more significant exchanges with the rest of the world through trade, education, leisure and globalization in general, increased interactions between European citizens and all those living in the EU, and the various cultures, languages, ethnic groups and religions in Europe and beyond (Ecotec, 2009). The EU's background was that the enlargement, the deregulation of employment laws and globalization have increased the 'multicultural' (in descriptive terms) character of many countries, adding to the number of languages, religions, and ethnic and cultural backgrounds. The EYID 2008 promoted the principle that Europe's great cultural diversity represents a unique advantage aimed at encouraging all those living in Europe to explore its rich cultural heritage and exploit opportunities to learn from different cultural traditions (Ecotec, 2009). The overall objectives were to promote ICD as a process that will strengthen respect for cultural diversity and help citizens to deal with complex realities in society, and the harmonious coexistence of different cultural identities and beliefs. Essentially, the EYID sought to increase the mutual understanding between peoples with different cultural backgrounds, leading to increased respect and tolerance using a range of activities, which in practice, appear to have been predominantly centred on cultural, educational and media-related activities, but could also encompass activities in the workplace and leisure spaces. Themes addressed through these activities included migration and integration, multilingualism and inter-faith dialogue. Essentially, therefore, it was about changing social attitudes through the process of cultural sharing and learning. This shows the extent to which the EYID was distinguished by a strong emphasis placed on awareness raising and the stimulation of thinking and debating around cross-cultural parameters. These initiatives were reinforced by the increase of conflictive relations among cultural groups as well as the threats related to security and terrorism. The increased tension and discrimination, lack of respect for diversity and the diminution of EU values were also part of the focus. Among the goals, the promotion of a shift from multiculturalism to interculturalism was announced, as well as an urgent need to foster a change in social attitude towards migrants.

One of the conclusions of the Ecotec Report is that the presence of ICD at the intra-national level was completely absent (Ecotec, 2009: 28–9). In terms of content, the concept of ICD itself, or the context within which it is embedded, varied significantly across the different policies, and in some cases there were indications that clear definitions were not established (Ecotec, 2009: 100). Among the outcomes, the report stresses the increase of general awareness of diversity, increase of participation and engagement, and increased respect and tolerance towards other cultures, and an even stronger sense of solidarity with people from other cultures. In terms of EU-level strategy and policy, most of the policy domains of education and training, culture, multilingualism, youth, sport and citizenship directly or indirectly address the ICD concept as one of their priority areas in the field.

2. THE DECISIVE TASK OF THE COUNCIL OF EUROPE IN PROVIDING A DISTINCTIVE EUROPEAN MEANING TO INTERCULTURAL CITIZENSHIP: THE CITY FRAMEWORK

As part of this first EU intercultural initiative, in 2005 the Council of Europe (CoE) moved to a coherent policy on ICD and in May 2008 it produced the White Paper on ICD (Council of Europe, 2008), which carried the EYID logo. Then it also penetrated the cultural policy, completely convinced that it is one of the best channels of ICD, together with education and a focus on young people. The link between the EYID and the 'Intercultural Cities' project, a joint action of the Council of Europe and the European Commission, appears to have been particularly strong, offering a coherent response to the important urban agenda. For example, the foreword written by the Mayor of The Hague and President of Eurocities, Mr J. van Aarsen, stated that

> Cities play a key role in terms of facilitating and supporting intercultural dialogue, promoting mutual understanding and acceptance, and overcoming barriers between different groups. They bring together different stakeholders at the local level and have a wide range of experience and knowledge to share regarding dialogue between cultures. (Eurocities, 2009: 2)

The task carried out by the Intercultural Cities (ICC) programme since 2008 contributed substantially then to draw this local lens of interculturalism in Europe. Its application to the cities is directly addressed, without any ambiguity. In fact, the ICC mantra is that the future of cities will be decided by how they manage diversity:

> One of the defining factors that will determine, over coming years, which cities flourish and which decline will be the extent to which they allow their diversity to be their asset, or their handicap. Whilst national and supranational bodies will continue to wield an influence it will increasingly be the choices that cities themselves make which will seal their future. (Council of Europe, 2008: 22)

This city-network strategy (at the time I am writing it has reached more than 135 cities all over Europe) is quite particular to Europe (for example, the Québécois approach is national-based), and has also been supported by the first books, coming from experts and consultants promoting interculturalism through the avenue of cities rather than states (Wood and Landry, 2008; Zapata-Barrero, 2015c). Since then, a practical step-by-step guide has served as the main document to frame the first internal debates among local policy makers, and an ICC index is being applied across Europe and further afield (Mexico, Rabat, Montreal, Tokyo) to benchmark its implementation.

This index gives us valuable primary information on how the intercultural policy paradigm is defined through 10 main dimensions. These dimensions constitute a comprehensive range of different areas of intervention for ensuring the conditions to foster relations among people from different backgrounds, including national citizens: assessment of city functions 'through an intercultural lens' (education, the public domain, housing and neighbourhoods, public services and civic administration, business and the economy, sport and the arts); urban safety; mediation and conflict resolution; languages; media strategy;

establishing an international policy for the city; evidence-based approach; intercultural awareness training; welcoming newcomers; and intercultural governance (which includes participation and representation).

The starting broad definition of interculturalism of the Council of Europe is based on dialogue promotion in the cities. In terms of the conceptual framework, ICD is understood in the White Paper as 'a process that comprises an open and respectful exchange of views between individuals and groups with different ethnic, cultural, religious and linguistic backgrounds and heritage, on the basis of mutual understanding and respect' (2008: 9). ICD requires then the freedom and ability to express oneself, as well as the willingness and capacity to listen to the views of others and also to be open to changing one's views.

Walking in this same argumentation path, the Council of Europe (2011b) has recently set out the ways in which they believe 'peaceful co-existence' can be achieved, strengthening the link between freedom and diversity. They set out 17 'guiding principles' for living together. These mainly revolve around legal rights, which apply equally to all, with an emphasis on citizenship and participation, in which people retain their distinctive cultural heritage, possibly hyphenated with nationality or faith. They also argue for early voting rights for migrants and for tolerant and respectful leadership. The cities are reinforced as one key actor for facilitating interculturalism. In this document it is again recognized that today, towns and cities are also home to a large majority of Europeans. Thus, it is within those parameters that the main encounters happen between people of different faiths, cultures or ethnic identities.

Another indicator of the particular relevance of ICD to cities is the 'European Network of cities for local integration policies for migrants (CLIP)' project, launched in September 2006,[2] which included a module on 'intercultural policies and intergroup relations' (Borkert et al., 2007; Lüken-Klaßen and Heckmann, 2010). This comes along with the United Nations (2015) report that stated that by 2050 the majority of the world's population will be living in cities, and human mobility and migration between urban areas will be central. And the answer these cities will give to diversity will also be central to understanding their economic development and their place in a global context.

There are also many documents that stress the importance of cities as a key actor for diversity management (e.g. European Commission, 2008a, 2008b, 2015). One of the first EU political documents making this 'city turn'

---

[2]Established by the European Foundation for the Improvement of Living and Working Conditions, the Council of Europe and the City of Stuttgart (www.eurofound.europa.eu/areas/populationandsociety/clip.htm).

explicit was the European Ministerial Conference on Integration (Zaragoza, 15–16 April 2010), held under the Spanish Presidency, which underlined once again the central role of local authorities when facing the challenges of applying intercultural and integration programmes. Specifically, the final declaration of the conference concluded:

> Considering that cities and their districts are privileged areas for fostering intercultural dialogue and for promoting cultural diversity and social cohesion, it is important for local governments to develop and obtain capacities to better manage diversity and to combat racism, xenophobia and all forms of discrimination. (European Commission, 2010: 7)

Finally, another key date is 15 January 2015, when the Committee of Ministers of the Council of Europe adopted a recommendation on the ICC approach, recognizing it as a way forward and recommending it to cities and governments. All these first documents drafting the European view of interculturalism share, then, the substantial idea that interculturalism is better implemented at the sub-state level. And the reasons for this are directly related to the fact that diversity management is better served by the administration that is close to the everyday life of citizens. These are the grounds of considering intercultural citizenship as local, with some implications following citizenship studies. We now go from a national-based to an urban-based view of citizenship.

3. THE URBAN FACE OF INTERCULTURAL CITIZENSHIP: SHAPING MICRO-POLITICS AND A POLICY OF PROXIMITY

All these European documents, despite their difference in emphasis, convey the same message to us: the link between intercultural citizenship and cities can be considered as being a European distinction. This involves that the citizenship focus adopts a rather urban face, which basically involves that citizenship is understood as being an inhabitant of the city independent of the national-origin. This urban view therefore follows the classical view of citizenship as being post-state and post-national. Here urban citizenship meets cosmopolitanism. In fact, the contextual framework that shapes the European view of interculturalism can only be understood as being at the crossroads of two dynamics that have been connected in practice. First, there is a common trend in Europe to go from a state- to a locally-centred approach in diversity policies, as cities are increasingly recognized not only as implementers of policies, but also as new players. Second, within this context, an increasing number of cities are shifting to the intercultural policy paradigm, due to the dissatisfaction that state multiculturalism has generated after several decades of narrative dominance. Intercultural cities are thus becoming a new orthodoxy for expressing a practical commitment to diversity-recognition.

The background idea of intercultural citizenship is, then, that contact between different people is politically and socially as relevant as the institutional recognition of cultural differences so widely defended by the methodological statism of multicultural citizenship. This move from macro-national to micro-local politics is at the foreground of what has been labelled the 'local turn' we are witnessing in migration studies (Caponio et al., 2018; Zapata-Barrero et al., 2017). Indeed, it is at the local level that the difficulties in implementing a *boundless multiculturalism* arise. It is at this micro-level that most of the diversity-related conflicts need a quick answer, which multicultural citizenship does not always manage to provide. In fact, we can venture to say that in these concrete micro-circumstances the multicultural citizenship narrative has even fuelled the same conflict it tried to solve.

Intercultural (urban) citizenship becomes in this way an attractive policy paradigm for local managers of migration-related diversity. It is much more connected to common people's concerns and best able to accommodate the specificities of local policies: pragmatism, proximity. It is also considered by some recent studies as a better policy tool to deal with economic crises (Caponio and Donatiello, 2017), superdiverse societies (Hadj Abdou and Geddes, 2017) and transnational realities of most people living in cities (Zapata-Barrero, 2018b).

To summarize, intercultural citizenship is lived day by day, with all its excitement and creativity, and all its problems and challenges. This also means that intercultural citizenship highlights a sense of place as a vital element in identity formation – and this can include the place where people live now and feel a sense of belonging through everyday practices in their neighbourhood (Hellgren, 2018). I would say that even if it is not its unique sphere of application, public spaces play a central role. It is in my view one of the forgotten areas of the multicultural citizenship paradigm. Public spaces ensure the best conditions of face-to-face relations (Chapter 7). The multicultural citizenship approach has difficulties reaching these micro-views, because it has deployed all its policy engineering to accommodate differences within the basic state structure. Put in other words, the multicultural citizenship paradigm fails to see the role that municipal policies can play in setting up physical spaces conducive to intercultural contact, which is likely to generate social cohesion, social capital and mutual understanding, paraphrasing Boucher and Maclure (2018).

Cities bear the main responsibility for ensuring that culturally diverse societies are open societies, in which people belonging to different cultural groups, including those who are perceived as recent arrivals or temporary residents, can feel at home and make their own contribution, in their own way, to the city's overall social cohesion. Thus, local authorities have a key role to play in the process of building peaceful relations between different people and of reducing tensions, which often arise along ethnic, religious or cultural fault lines.

What becomes clear from the beginning of this chapter is that intercultural citizenship implies an urban citizen. This also involves a development within citizenship studies, since equality of rights (citizenship liberal dimension), sense of belonging and community-building (the communitarian dimension of citizenship) and participation in the public space (the citizenship republican dimension) are thought to be applied at the city level rather than at the state level, where the traditional legal-national view of citizenship prevails (we will go into these different conceptions of citizenship in Chapter 7). In this sense, intercultural citizenship charts the course, the focus, the horizon and the direction of small-scale programmes, and is becoming a strategic municipal project. Implementation areas can have a variable focal length within the territorial limits of the city: as an overall city project, and on a smaller scale, at the level of districts, and even streets and concrete public settings (market, playground, etc.), particular projects either thematic and topic-oriented or targeting particular profiles of people (young people, women, artists, intergenerational projects, etc.) or seeking to foster determinate values, beliefs and life prospects.

4. ORIGINS AND FIRST PREMISES OF THE INTERCULTURAL POLICY NARRATIVE IN SCHOLARLY DEBATES

Following Brubaker's (2012) useful distinction, interculturalism has previously been a category of practice rather than a category of analysis.[3] One could even say that the *notion* existed before the *concept*. For instance, in 1997 the city of Barcelona opted to call its policy 'intercultural' as a result of dissatisfaction with the existing multicultural/assimilationist models in Europe (Zapata-Barrero, 2017c). Essentially, this was justified because multiculturalism was seen to be distant from the mainstream policy and assimilationism did not respect legitimate cultural practices of certain groups. From the very beginning, a focus on

---

[3]Brubaker (2012) says in the interview we have quoted: 'It's important to distinguish between categories of analysis – the categories that social scientists use – and categories of practice that are used in everyday social and political life.'

promoting contact rather than separation, on working towards immigrants' inclusion and on devising policies concentrating on immigrants within the basic mainstream structure of public services, was put forward as an integration policy that responded better to current views. This intercultural policy was also theorized in other parts of Europe as an inclusion policy with the central purpose of preventing socio-economic exclusion.[4]

The first theoretical articulation (interculturalism as a category of analysis) came from experts Wood and Landry (2008) (not from academia, as was the case with the multicultural citizenship paradigm), whose urban intercultural philosophy influenced the intercultural city programme of the Council of Europe.

Coming mainly from urban, social management and business studies,[5] but also from social psychology[6] and a burgeoning literature from education studies,[7] it has penetrated policy debates on diversity and immigration studies only very recently.[8] The first promoters brought with them a different concept of diversity, which was not considered by either multiculturalist or civic nationalists: the concept of *diversity advantage*[9] (we will discuss the contents of this concept in Chapter 8). This notion of diversity as a potential resource and a source of opportunities is path-breaking in current post-M debates, and absent in multiculturalism from the very beginning.

Cantle's writings are another valuable European source, illustrating a less constructivist focus and drawing on a much more social and cosmopolitan strand of interculturalism. It also has a particular view of diversity, probably close to the preventive concerns described in Putnam's (2007) seminal work. That is, diversity

---

[4] See Borkert et al. (2007); Caponio and Borkert (2010); Caponio and Ricucci (2015); Lüken-Klaßen and Heckmann (2010). This last work provides an overview as to how the debate was introduced by EU institutions.

[5] See, among others, Blommaert and Verschueren (1998); Bloomfield and Bianchini (2004); Festenstein (2005); Gundara and Jacobs (2000); Hussein et al. (2006); Festenstein (2005); Page (2007); Sandercock (2004); Sze and Powell (2004); Wood (2004); Wood and Landry (2008); Zachary (2003).

[6] Hewstone (2015); Pettigrew and Tropp (2008, 2013).

[7] Catarci and Fiorucci (2016); Gundara (2000); Gundara and Portera (2008); Peters and Besley (2012); Tupas (2014).

[8] See Barrett (2013); Cantle (2012); Lüken-Klaßen and Heckmann (2010); Meer and Modood (2012); Taylor (2012); Zapata-Barrero (2013, 2015c).

[9] The concept of diversity advantage has been introduced by the UK think tank Comedia, directed by Wood (2004) and mainly inspired by Zachary's (2003) seminal work.

without policy intervention can be a source of conflict and can increase the socio-economic disadvantages of diverse people. The notion of conflict related to diversity has to be understood in a broad sense as encompassing racism, poverty and social exclusion (Cantle, 2012: 102). In this sense, we can also see that there is a certain preventive dimension in the intercultural citizenship paradigm. This second more preventive view of diversity has been articulated by Cantle (2012: 30). He was responsible for a report on the British government's concern regarding local riots stemming from social unrest in northern towns in August 2011 (Bradford, Burnley and Oldham; see more details on his website: http://tedcantle.co.uk/). These events directly linked social conflicts with the failure of British multicultural policy. His book *Community Cohesion* (2008) articulated these ideas against the multicultural citizenship paradigm and argued against the promotion of 'parallel lives' between communities that had little in common and no contact with each other. The debate between multiculturalism and interculturalism in Britain quickly took this contextual framework and featured the contrasting views of Modood and Cantle on how to understand the place of diversity and culture in integration policies.[10]

The idea of 'community cohesion' then comes into the debate, as a new normative driver together with the diversity advantage promoted by Wood and Landry, and the view of interculturalism as a tool for negotiation between Diversity and Unity, *à la* Bouchard. The central claim of the intercultural citizenship paradigm here is that there is a need to go beyond the ethnicization of politics and the very concrete concept of culture related to national identity and race. This post-national and post-racial view of culture is certainly a direct critique of multicultural citizenship's core assumptions, allowing us to centre the policy on common bonds, which must prevail over differences as a premise on which to formulate policies. This does not mean that intercultural citizenship focuses on sameness as a criterion driving policy legitimation, as multicultural citizenship has rightly criticized (Parekh, 2000). With this, it emphasizes what is (or can be) shared between people or groups, rather than exhibiting what is different and 'must be recognised and respected' among people who see each other in terms of otherness. By the way, it is under this focus that intercultural citizenship shows its most humanitarian face. This initial focus is responsible for pointing out the common humanity that emerges from contact. Intercultural citizenship not only suggests the acceptance of principles of equal rights, values and abilities, but also supports the development of policies to promote diversity exchanges, collaboration and communication with people sharing the same

---

[10]For a good introduction to the debate, see Antonsich (2016).

territory. Furthermore, intercultural citizenship is an approach that sees difference as a positive resource that can enrich a society (Titley, 2012).

Promoters of the intercultural paradigm are fully aware that shared practices and relations can be constrained by inequality and asymmetrical power relations, and by the lack of a minimum level of common public culture. It is probably at this point that interculturalism shows its most demanding side, requiring the appropriate conditions for inter-personal relations and the mitigation of risk at contact zones that could wrongfully become conflict zones, particularly in vulnerable areas where tensions between communities prevail.[11] Probably the added value of the intercultural citizenship is that in promoting contact between people from different backgrounds it also helps to develop intercultural values such as trust, common understanding and what we may call a *culture of diversity*, which essentially means going beyond the simple fact that cities are currently diverse, in order to discuss how diversity is being incorporated into public and civic culture, at the level of both institutional structures and routines. This means re-designing institutions and policies in all fields to treat diversity as a potential resource and a public good that needs to be distributed, and not as a nuisance to be contained. This *culture of diversity* can be seen as a by-product of what in the recent work of Matejskova and Antonsich (2015) is called governance *through* diversity rather than governance *of* diversity. The *through* indicates that diversity does not exist apart from politics, but needs to be incorporated within governance (2015: 3), the incorporation of diversity in political parties probably being the first step (Zapata-Barrero et al., 2018), with further research required for other pillars of society (schools, police, administration, etc.).

An example of an intercultural concern when requesting citizenship tests could be whether diversity is incorporated as a common value to be respected or still treated as something that falls outside Unity. This is why I define this *culture of diversity* through three main standards: Diversity-recognition, Diversity-participation and Diversity management (Zapata-Barrero, 2014: 68). In this claim of incorporating diversity in all spheres of the society, the intercultural citizenship paradigm can also fight to include diversity within the cherished notion of 'common value' articulating the civic-national policy narrative. The civic integration policy speaks about a culture of citizenship (Mouritsen, 2012) rather than a culture of diversity, and then it seems to still place diversity outside rather than inside mainstream society.

---

[11] These power relations between people and socio-economic contrasts are fully addressed in the work of Cantle (2012) for instance. It is an area that certainly needs deeper examination.

3

INTERCULTURAL TURN IN EUROPE: IN A DIVERSE EUROPE, WHAT DOES 'EUROPEANNESS' MEAN TODAY?

INTRODUCTION: THE EUROPEAN UNION'S GOVERNANCE OF MIGRATION-RELATED DIVERSITY – AN ON-GOING PROJECT

Europe's cultural, ethnic, linguistic and religious diversity will increase in a transformative way in the coming years and decades. It has already transformed all the European diversity social geography, up to the point that the 'we' and 'others', the majority and minority frameworks, in spite of framing most of the national-state narratives, have real empirical difficulties in grounding the European Union (EU). The policy reality also tells us that the current self-understanding of EU is still disconnected from the changing diverse sociodemographic landscape of the European continent. This leads us to argue that the crisis of Europe today is related to its self-representation as it has been constructed since its foundation. The debate on diversity is still happening within national silos. Seen from a migration-related diversity lens, the EU political project remains a patchwork of many national diversity management approaches. Most states have adopted a national-civic narrative incorporating citizenship tests and linking their citizenship regimes to the diversity debate (Jacobs and Rea, 2007; Michalowski, 2011), but these same countries also follow other multicultural and intercultural policy approaches at sub-state levels. Clearly there is no European approach to migration-related diversity governance, because the EU has left this business to Member States. This gap has even become a category of analysis. For example, some studies argue that the way the national community is constructed with respect to cultural diversity influences citizens'

readiness to identify with a broader community characterized by high cultural diversity such as Europe (Schlenker-Fischer, 2010).

The current scenario is indeed that Europe witnesses a plurality of approaches to diversity management. This fact symbolizes more a history of conflict and friction, a driver of fragmentation and division among Member States rather than a history of union. Europe is simply losing a golden opportunity to build a political body that incorporates cultural, ethnic and religious diversity as a constitutive part of its common history. Ethnic minorities, people who may be European citizens in the coming years or long-term residents of Europe, having moved to Europe two or three generations ago, put the European project and identity-building process to the test. Without incorporating migration-related diversity, European identity is simply a half-empty bottle and may lose one great part of its potential for transformation and innovation.

In this chapter I will defend interculturalism as one of the core values of Europe that needs to be reassessed. It could be the new flag of European identity substituting for the old-fashioned one based nowadays on a false descriptor between 'Unity in Diversity', that legitimizes rather than solves inequalities and power relations related to migration diversity. This 'intercultural turn' has already been assessed as a changing paradigm for Europe (Zapata-Barrero, 2017d). I will concentrate now on the arguments that support the answers to why interculturalism could be a driver to reboot the same European identity.

This chapter will have four main streams, which will be interconnected through a consequence-based framework of analysis. First, I want to underline that the current identity crisis is related to the core ontological values that make Europe a collective project. Second, I will justify the need to open a reflection on how the EU building process is missing the historical opportunity to include migrants within its own European identity-building process, with the help of several empirical studies on European identity formation. The third stream will signal the danger that if things remain the same, the EU could become a machine generating frustrated second-generations migrants. Then I will conclude, as a fourth stream, on the need to incorporate interculturalism as one of the greatest and most distinctive values that can drive European identity towards the future.

1. EU ONTOLOGICAL CRISIS: IN SEARCH OF A WE-EUROPEAN, WHICH INCLUDES MIGRATION-RELATED DIVERSITY

The process of European integration has braked hard and is currently on standby, finding itself in an unprecedented crisis since its foundation. Europe has been divided, broken, fragmented, stalled by internal geopolitical unprecedented conflicts of interests, which have been ungovernable with refugees. These are some of the key panels that define the current historical moment. The EU is undergoing a life-threatening crisis today on the values that drove its political project, which are directly related to European citizenship, free movement, and European post-national politics. Most probably there are other drivers, but one conundrum that may explain the recent boiling point Europe has reached is directly related to the incapacity to give a collective answer to diversity-recognition. Moreover, the primary reason why xenophobic discourses worry Europe is that there is a certain awareness that xenophobia is not a favourable factor for European identity (Roeder, 2011) and even nurtures Euro-scepticism.

We are in a period of the 'broken ideal of European citizenship' (Zapata-Barrero, 2016a), where even the values of free movement find limits at the internal level, among cross-Member States' movements and EU citizens. It is striking that for more than one decade the debate has mostly been focused on managing flows and obsessing about security, with the aggravating growing fear of the entrance of populist parties into the political system and governance with clear purposes against diversity. For some, the urgent human imperative is to save people from drowning at sea. For others, it is the xenophobic rush to put up fences and push families away. There are at least two interconnected drivers of this ontological European identity crisis, and as I will argue, these drivers are also part of the process to reboot the European project.

The first one comes from below, at the national-state level, namely the strong link found between Euro-scepticism and anti-immigration and narratives against diversity (Leconte, 2015). The second one comes from inside Europe as a political construction: the lack of diversity-recognition, or the fact that diversity is still used today as a euphemistic category to speak about 'the others'. As I have already stressed, there is always a subtle semantic process when those who define diversity fail to include themselves within this category. Diversity is always considered by European standards to refer to non-Europeans. Europe has constructed diversity categories related to dimensions of race, ethnicity, religion and language as being at the origin of social polarization and political conflicts. Because the main sources generating meaning to the European identity are the states, in the process of building Europe as a political entity, within the core European citizenship, Europe has never had a pro-active view of diversity related to migrants.

However, there have been from the very beginning many voices claiming that there were a number of people labelled migrants in European states who were ignored in the EU building process, and that this group must be constitutively recognized as being part of the European construction. We can see this neglect has been evident when we analyse the policy and institutional narrative that has governed the EU political construction: the migration dossier has always been placed within the broader security and justice agenda, together with drug trafficking, terrorism and criminals. The main challenges in the EU political foundation have been concerning how to ensure freedom of movement inside Europe for EU citizens, as a condition for fostering the Union's identity, whilst avoiding the fact that the internal border freedom does not affect the stability of national states. Here lies the Schengenland process and the Fortress Europe narrative (Geddes, 2003). Sharing this diagnosis, some voices have formulated the need to include migrants within the European citizenship project without the simultaneous acquisition of national citizenship in any Member State (Becker, 2004). By extending European citizenship to migrants, new modes of political and social participation, as well as economic mobility, could significantly enhance migrant integration in a variety of contexts. But these claims remain in the void, even if the arguments put forward seem, to me, highly coherent, and can even announce a cosmopolitan Europe, as some have also claimed (Beck and Grande, 2014) more than one decade ago.

Let me give an additional historical statement. If European nation-states can flag an argument to justify the difficulties they have in managing diversity today, it is because of a social dynamic that did not exist during the state-building origin; the EU, as a political entity, cannot use the same argument since migration-related diversity was already known and discussed in 1992, when the Maastricht Treaty opened the avenue of European citizenship and the political union-building process. Migration-related diversity already belonged to European societies; it was already a policy and academic debate that focused on how to integrate migrants and manage diversity. We can also add that one of the requirements to enter into the European project even before the beginning of the political process was to have a migration law and policy. Spain, for instance, reacted quickly to this constraint and formulated its first Aliens Law in 1985, just a year before its ratification. The same compulsory demand was requested for all other new Eastern States. Thereby, Europe has always interpreted the presence of migrants and the diversity dynamics they provoke under a methodological statism. Most scholars have even signalled that migrants have not been considered as being a constitutive part of European *demos*, even if they were fully aware of its *de facto* existence. Today this neglect is unjustified as we are in a much more complex scenario, where there is no clear dividing line between who is national and who is not, with second and third generations of migrants, with the presence of people who are still considered as migrants in the short-term collective social memory, in spite of now being part of the

European *demos* (I speak about most of the newcomers into European citizenship after the enlargement of the EU at the beginning of this century).

It is true that a realistic analysis of diversity incorporation in the EU must face the argument that to include migration-related diversity could incite further resistance from EU citizens to support Europe, but this can only be a short-term reaction. This is also evidence that this process cannot be done without an accompanying policy process of socialization of European citizens and extensive European campaigns that recognize that Europe is diverse not only in respect of national identities related to Member States, but also in respect of migration-related diversity.

This proposal will be the outcome of my diagnosis: we are now in an ontological situation where the markers of European identity need to be reassessed. The so-called 'normalisation' of ethno-national political parties with anti-immigrant narratives into the mainstream political system is directly related to the way the European project has been drafted – without taking into account migrants-related diversity categories. My argument tries to reverse the direction of this equation: the problem is not that immigration is fuelling these populist discourses, but rather that immigration and diversity, as they have not been considered in the state-centric European identity formation, as they have been neglected, are now influencing Euro-scepticisms. And this is because – I reach now the end of my argument – we are missing a European value: interculturalism.

Adopting this intercultural lens involves having direct awareness of the European motto 'Unity in Diversity', which has been formulated under state and national parameters, and not within the parameters of categories related to migration diversity. It follows that to achieve this horizon, Europe understood, as a political project, that it needed to free itself from its methodological national-statism's iron jacket. And what needs to be done first is the EU to recognize that diversity as related to migration is an integrative part of the We-European population, which will involve a process of diversity-recognition in all the structures of the EU's political fabric. This recognition is also the premise and condition *sine qua non* to incorporate interculturalism as one of the main flags of the new Europe and a new driver of European identity formation.

2. MIGRANTS AS PIONEERS OF EUROPE? HOW MIGRANTS CAN HELP TO REBOOT EUROPEAN IDENTITY

The EU has always been a spectator of the different states' diversity approaches (multiculturalism, assimilation or national-civism or a mixture of them depending on the level of government). This methodological nationalism at the core of the EU fabric has also meant that most of the theoretical frameworks governing diversity debates at the national level are produced at the European level. I mean basically the majority/minority framework. Who are majority and minority if we take the diversity of European society seriously? This question is probably inadequate, since it will reproduce political cleavages and power relations and institutionalize inequalities, which are precisely the outcomes we need to avoid when speaking about diversity. This forces us to also redraft most of the European vocabulary towards migrants. Immigrants are defined clearly as third-country nationals, that is as non-nationals of Member States, rather than as non-Europeans. In fact, the perception of the 'other' as it is reproduced by national states involves the legitimization of some views that precisely contravene the recognition of diversity we are claiming as a premise for rebooting European identity. For instance, if a German does not manage to see a second-generation Turk as German this means that neither will they see the same person as European, even if this same person has acquired German nationality and hence has a European passport. The idea of Europeanness is always perceived from the 'us/other' national side. So, and again, the fundamental problem still lies in the national dependence in the making of European identity!

Let's put the argument directly. It has been argued during these past years that European citizens are the pioneers of Europe (Favell and Recchi, 2009); this is because they are the ones who could enjoy the freedom of cross-border mobility and maximize the rights associated with European citizenship. This spatial argument is a mechanism to shape EU identity; there is an assumed premise and it is time to bring it to light: it is neither movement that shapes European identity nor European citizenship by itself, but instead it is what this presupposes: contact between people, between nationals of different European states, having intercultural experiences. Because EU immigrants constitute the group of EU citizens that makes the most use of the advantages provided by the EU, such as EU citizenship, they are expected to endorse the largest European identity (Rother and Nebe, 2009). My view is that this debate misses highlighting that it is the outcome of movement that matters, not just mobility alone. In other words, if I move to another state and do so in isolation, without interacting with others, I will never develop a European identity. The movement alone cannot be a driver, but a facilitator to promote contact, which is *de facto* the main driver of European identity.

In general, this debate has been grounded using Deutsch's (1966) seminal work on the construction of national identity based on free spatial mobility. The same author insists that the potential for nurturing a common identity can only be realized via increased transactions and common experiences among citizens. In fact, when mobility becomes a *habitus*, in Bourdieusian terms (1984: 466), transnational interactions become the norm and then diversity could even become a public culture. This bottom-up and constructivist approach of European identity formation (Recchi, 2012) is what the intercultural strategy as a policy mechanism can institutionalize as a norm. This sociological approach insists that numerous social interactions across borders within the EU are associated with higher levels of European consciousness (Kuhn, 2015). The cross-mobility not only can be seen as a necessary mechanism for European identity formation, but for what it could foster: knowledge-exchange, inter-personal experiences, interdependencies, interactions among people from different cultures, national identities, religions, etc.

Moreover, social psychology's contact theory on tradition working identity formation (e.g. Gaertner et al., 1993) underlines that contact must be positive in order for the interaction to contribute to a common sense of belonging. Thus, positive social contacts with other Europeans can transmit a sense of belonging, and thus enhance European identification (Teney et al., 2016). But the literature also stresses one distinctive variable that may affect immigrants or citizens with a migrant background: discrimination. This factor may seriously and negatively affect the sense of belonging in general and the European identification in particular, even if positive contact and experience occurs. This also leads some to frame the European identification of migrants with regard to social and cultural distance in relation to European nationals. Going deeper in the analysis, Teney et al. (2016: 2188) also insist that we cannot simply postulate that the more mobile migrants are, the more they feel European, but instead this relationship is likely to be moderated depending on the country of origin and its historical relation with the EU. We can even apply Bruter's (2005) arguments, which are initially destined for Europeans, to migrants: the degree to which people recognize themselves both in the EU political project and also in its cultural, political and philosophical values and norms, fosters European identity. In this sense, to put a straightforward argument: Muslim immigrants might find it difficult to identify with a conception of Europe in which Eurocentric visions of a white and Christian Europe are still dominant. The European public narrative is still conducted by homogenized representations of Muslim populations without giving much consideration to the heterogeneous silos and movements within the same Muslim population throughout Europe (Cinalli and Giugni, 2013). But some studies also show that belonging to a religious affiliation that differs from the dominant religious tradition of the EU does not seem to affect the level of European identity.

So here again 'migrants as pioneers of Europe' may have a role in this process of rebooting the European project so that it includes migration-related diversity. Another important finding in the literature (Teney et al., 2016) is the relevance of distinguishing transnational social practices from the physical crossing of borders from the others. Accordingly, transnational social practices that imply spatial mobility (such as visits to the country of origin) are indeed significantly associated with European identity among immigrants.

An additional argument is that the inclusion of migrants in the European integration process has always been seen as a democratization debate. The argument is simple; recognizing European intercultural citizenship would help further the democratization of European governance (Becker, 2004). As migration issues are mainly governed under national rules, this makes it clearly difficult to view migrants as part of European democratic society. There are even many inconsistencies put forward by many scholars (Bauböck, 2019). Latin-Americans can be European citizens in two years following the Spanish citizenship regime, but will need more years in whatever European Member country. Or as Bauböck (1997) put it some decades ago: suppose a family from Turkey splits up in the migration process, with a brother going to Germany and a sister to Sweden. After five years the sister becomes naturalized and thereby acquires EU citizenship. She is now free to join her brother in Germany, where she will enjoy not only free access to employment but also the franchise for local and European Parliament elections. Her brother, who has lived in Germany all the time, will remain in a considerably weaker position. The list of incoherencies can be longer and show how necessary it is to think of Europe from the point of view of migrants.

To summarize, the matrix clustering all these arguments is always the assumption that contact matters, that personal exchange's promotion is what makes identity formation work. Applied to the European identity, this means that only by recognizing migration-related diversity as a constitutive part of its history can the EU legitimize the promotion of intercultural exchanges; and it is only through fostering these encounters that the EU can redress the dynamics of identity formation. It is intercultural contact that shapes European identity and the sense of European community.

3. CAN THE EU SURVIVE WITHOUT A SENSE OF EU COMMUNITY? THE EU AS MACHINERY GENERATING FRUSTRATED SECOND-GENERATION MIGRANTS

A complementary way to enter into the same story circle that migrants are pioneers of Europe is that they force Europe to define itself when dealing with migration-related diversity issues. The first path is the numerous recent surveys that share the conclusion that migrants are sometimes more EU supporters than national citizens. The combination of this fact, without a correspondence in European institutions to recognize their differentness and their right to European citizenship, can revert in the short term to a lesser Europeanness of second- and third-generation migrants. In fact, migrants are probably the sector of the population that has developed a sense of European identity even before national citizens. If we review the recent trends of migrant attitudes towards European identity, the drivers of this affiliation are multifaceted. Some say it is a cost-benefit logic of thought. As Fligstein (2010) argues, European identification strongly depends on the extent to which individuals benefit from the EU. This interest-based approach sometimes appears to be higher than the legal barriers and limited access to the mainstream society (Roeder, 2011). But this European identity is frustrated when the EU only implements their values to manage diversity at the national level. Migrants have more difficulties than European citizens in moving between states and have a different set of rights and duties, and their opportunities depend on which states they are in, so basically their Europeanism is frustrated due to this methodological statist barrier in the making of Europe. Migrants are simply without European references.

Studies on European identity have flourished over the past 20 years in political science and sociology (Triandafyllidou and Gropas, 2015) and there is a general consensus that there has been neglect in incorporating non-EU immigrants in such studies (Teney et al., 2016). It is really only recently that European identity studies have begun to incorporate the variable of migrants and even compare it with national citizens. Even though these studies have been done on different scales and sites there is little divergence of findings. The summary is not only that migrants have a sense of Europeanness, but that in spite of having difficulties developing a sense of belonging at the national level, they feel they are part of European society. This gap between migrant EU identity and a *de facto* exclusion from the European *demos* is seen as one of the paradoxes that may push migrants into social frustrations (Teney et al., 2016). Legal exclusions do not lead to less European identification. These works also show one trend, that people with more than one identity, transnational or multiple affiliations, tend to be more European, independently of whether they feel they are treated fairly or not (Roeder, 2011).

So, migrants can only be pioneers of Europe if Europe facilitates their mobility and reduces their frustration at always being considered third-country nationals and at being increasingly and disproportionately predisposed to becoming victims of discrimination in different areas of society without European protections. It could be this factor that may cause the permanence of this paradox. As Teney et al.'s (2016: 2183) work shows, even if the UK is known for its Euroscepticism, British Asians (both generations) are more pro-European than the white British respondents, and British Asians' national identity is not negatively correlated with their European identity, while it is negatively correlated for white British respondents.

I have myself defended that in the substantial debate on the definition of the external European borders, there are many difficulties in seeing where Europe, as a political community, lies (Zapata-Barrero, 2009). At the border control and flow-management level, as a Union of states, the EU has developed some policies and harmonized certain approaches related to visa policies, return policies and even detention camps. Speaking about European identity is to speak about the possibility of a European community (Castiglione, 2009). In this sense migrants are pioneers of Europe, since they provoke the need to develop a common view of European borders, a common migration policy, and they are drivers of the European sense of (state-)community.

As I have shown from different avenues of argumentation, the same conclusion arises: incorporating migration-related diversity into the EU fabric is still a pending issue that can only be done if the EU is detached from the nationalstate cement where it has been from its origin. It is this national methodology driving EU fabric that is in crisis, not the ambition to reboot European identity under other parameters. As I will conclude in this chapter, interculturalism could be a distinctive value to reappraise a new historical phase of European identity formation.

4. FINAL REMARKS: INTERCULTURALISM, A DISTINCTIVE VALUE OF EUROPEAN IDENTITY

The intercultural dialogue year in 2008 made it clear that interculturalism was understood under the international relations lens, both as a cross-state relation and also as a cross-regional relation between Europe and other regions in the world. The third dimension, that is as inter-personal relations independently of ethnic, cultural and religious background, was simply left aside (see Chapter 2). The fact we are now defending interculturalism as a European value and mechanism for European identity formation belongs, then, to the cosmopolitan and post-ethnic trend to detach European identity from the iron jacket of national identity. This is quite revolutionary, but it really needs to be done in order to reboot European identity today, since the crisis of values is related to the lack of consideration of this more sociological dimension of diversity. What I am defending is the value of intercultural promotion that goes beyond and transforms the identity of the community hitherto supposed uniform (Staiger, 2009).

The recognition of diversity at the EU social and institutional levels can act as an antidote against any kind of fundamentalism, of the tendency that some would want to impose a worldview on others. A real diverse society is one where no one can impose their own cultural vision upon others. It is a safe bet, but one that politicians will probably not endorse easily, since they are too stuck on short-termism. Nor will high-minded reminders of European charters be enough. If a promising dynamic can be created, it must come from interculturalism, as a mechanism for fostering a culture of diversity and the restart of European identity formation. Now is the time to launch a pan-European view on migration-related diversity-recognition. And it is important to include interculturalism as one of the core drivers. As far as I know, only Pinxten et al. (2007: 693) put interculturalism so clearly as an answer to his guiding question, incorporating a time frame dimension to the intercultural policy paradigm: how can Europeans construct the EU so that it survives as a durable structure that will guarantee a democratic society of equal opportunities to its citizens? He probably is one of the first scholars to be so straightforward in introducing the intercultural question into the EU identify formation: 'We think that the capability of dealing with differences in a durable manner, based on equality and freedom, can be fostered by helping people develop their capacity for intercultural negotiation' (2007: 695). He argues that intercultural relations within Europe can ensure stable relationships. The fact that the population is becoming more and more mixed makes the development of intercultural negotiation skills increasingly important. The capacity to live with and respect diversity can be reconciled with the values of freedom and equality only by conceptualizing the EU as a space for intercultural relations.

If we accept as a premise that European identity is based on shared values such as human rights, equality of rights, autonomy and free will, cross-states freedom of movement, solidarity and social rights, why cannot migrants without any national-state restrictions enjoy these values?

In this case the crisis today of European identity is directly related not only to the values, but to the mechanism the EU has put forward to ensure these values, which is why one mechanism could be intercultural citizenship. Interculturalism as a method applied at the EU level could be a perfect European citizenship learning process.

In fact, viewed more closely, the notion of interculturalism has always been at the heart of Europe. But it has always been taken for granted and its scope varied. As a political project everything is in relation in Europe. If we want to see distinctive dimensions of Europe, it is no doubt via the complex web of contact between people, between cities, between states that constitute Europe. Without contact promotion there will never be the European project. So, what happens when contact is not between states or between national-member people, but between people whatever their origin, their statutes and legal situation in whatever national state? If Europe is an open space where 'everything is in relation' (Kastoryano, 2009: 18), then this must also apply to a Europe of diverse people. It is precisely the whole set of these relations that leads to a redefinition of universality, particularity, nationality and citizenship. This nuclear core (contact) of Europe is what drives its values and principles: mobility, free movement, etc. Hence, Unity in Diversity will acquire another scope so that it includes people instead of states or governments. This European motto will reach other people who were set aside and become really a lemma for inclusion rather than exclusion.

This intercultural principle of rebooting the European project will be much more appropriate to current diversity realities in Europe, and can be corroborated by current research findings. It is no longer controversial among scholars, and increasingly among policy makers, that individuals hold multiple social identities. The challenge can be formulated as follows: how does one go beyond the view of European identity as a construct of national-state identities instead of simply multiple identities of its population, be these identities connected to the state or various states (as transnational identities), or simply with no specific national state, but to a cosmopolitan identity? Europe as a space of coexistence of multiple identities still needs to be defined, and it is here that the intercultural citizenship paradigm may be a method to connect people in the European shared space. We can even say of those people living in the EU without recognizing diversity, and without a predisposition to interact with other cultures, that it is difficult to call them Europeans, since Europeaness is built on diversity-recognition, a culture of diversity and intercultural behaviour. This multiple identity approach of Europe can also lead to an interesting debate on the multiple ways to frame the relations between inter-diversity categories. These different strands of identities can be conceptualized in at least three ways (Herrmann et al., 2004: 8). Instead of the separate or exclusive approach, which only works in very exceptional cases, overlapping multiple identities or nested ones, conceived in a concentric circle like Russian Matryoshka dolls, prevail. But the marble-cake model seems to be more akin to the intercultural Europe. This approach articulated by Risse (2002) implies that identities can also be inseparably mixed with one another so that the various components of an individual's identity are seen to mesh and blend into one another. This means that the various components of an individual's identity cannot be neatly separated on different levels as both concepts of nestedness and of cross-cutting identities imply. What if identity components influence each other, mesh and blend into each other (Risse, 2004: 251–2)? What if my self-understanding as German/Moroccan inherently contains aspects of Europeanness? Can we really separate out a Catalan from a European identity? There are also some empirical studies that show liberal cosmopolitan pictures (Citrin and Sides, 2004) according to which identification with Europe increases tolerance of foreigners and decreases xenophobia. Thereby, an intercultural Europe can also reduce the space of one of the main concerns today: the consolidation of xenophobic anti-diversity narratives.

These multiple national identities and affiliations are the basis of post-ethnic Europe (Martiniello, 2001) and of the cosmopolitan vision of Europe (Beck and Grande, 2014). This involves a rejection of ethnic and racial ascriptions in favour of free choice. This way it promotes solidarity between individuals with different backgrounds. And finally, it leaves the door open for the inclusion of new collective identities. In Martiniello's words (2001: 66): a post-ethnic society would be one in which the opportunity to express one's ethnic options would be equally distributed among all individuals, something that is definitely not the case today in the EU fabric. The intercultural Europe is a post-ethnic Europe in the sense that not only will it encourage freely chosen identities and in this way reject ascribed or imposed identities, but it will respect individual autonomy. Together with interculturalism, solidarity is also a great value produced by cultural exchange. If we assume that the European space embraces people with various ethnic, racial, economic, cultural and religious categories, this cooperation between individuals becomes a value that needs to be promoted in order to foster European identity. The idea of solidarity, for instance, has been at the essence of cooperation between Member States, and even within each Member State at the core of welfare regimes, but not among diverse individuals (Zapata-Barrero, 2018a).

The capacity to live with and respect diversity can be reconciled with the values of freedom and equality only by conceptualizing the EU as a space for intercultural contacts. This will allow us to deal with the factual diversity in which we are living. This bottom-up approach and constructivist view of European identity formation is one that says it is through behaviours and actions, rather than from a supposed essence, culturalist and civilization or top-down approach, that the European identity can be shaped. Finally, interculturalism as a value is also a method for building identity by making society. The building of a European identity can only proceed on the basis of the acceptance of its multi-ethnic, multi-religious and multi-cultural character, and this acceptance needs a material basis in immigration and naturalization policies, in the education system and in the openness of the media, and of cultural institutions for the diversity of cultural expressions.

4

THE BUSINESS CARD OF INTERCULTURAL CITIZENSHIP: DISTINCTIVE FEATURES

INTRODUCTION: INTERCULTURAL CITIZENSHIP IN TIMES OF DIVERSE COMPLEXITY

Scholarly migration debates signal that there are now new trends that have become the norm, such as the fact that people have multiple and transnational identities without being really willing to rank them. Also, the need to formulate policies that target all the population and do not contribute to consolidate a social differentiation among people by specific policies, as has been the rule during the multicultural citizenship period. There is a general view that diversity policies are also needed by national citizens, not only by migrants and citizens of migrant origin.

The fact is that there is not a universal ranking of identities. Identities arise in given practices and according to determinate contexts. If I go to see a football match my supportive identity will come first, but in other contexts, other identities would emerge first. To rank identities without taking context into account is what certain multiculturalists seem to assume, as if there were primary identities that are permanently active in any given context.[1] Identity is a place-making process. In the same vein, a diversity of loyalties amidst growing global mobility and increasing cross-border human movement is becoming the norm.

---

[1] It is true that some multiculturalists recognize that some identities are more salient or pervasive than others and more important to their bearers (see Modood, 2007: 108–10).

These new patterns tell us that that diversity becomes a complex term. This basically means both that there is not a 'solitary' root cause of most of the conflicts that may arise in the process of diversity incorporation, and that there are still many unsolved uncertainties that govern our decision-makers, most of them related to the growing banality of racism and xenophobic narratives, and the restraints there are to ensure a real structure of opportunities for those who are still seen as 'different' and as 'others'.

The new debate on super-diversity also belongs to this track of incorporating complexity into diversity studies (Vertovec, 2014), as does the literature on network societies arising from the seminal work of Castells (1999), showing that the question of personal identity is much more connected to how people relate to each other, rather than the traditional 'Who am I?' based on where I was born (territory) or who my parents are (descent). We can even add some generational arguments. People already socialized into diverse societies are facing the challenge of reconciling national and city identities with different cultural strands and multiple identities in everyday social life (Crul et al., 2012).

The multicultural citizenship debate faces difficulties incorporating the practical implications of these new trends. It has a view of culture in national homogeneous terms, and places it in a power relationship within the basket of majority-national citizens. Robins and Aksoy (2016: 13) reminded us of this recently when Kymlicka (1995: 118, 94) recognized that he was 'using "a culture" as synonymous with "a nation" or "a people"', claiming that 'political life has an inescapably national dimension'. We know perfectly well that Kymlicka defines national community as 'societal culture', which includes the history, traditions and conventions that go along with the host society (Kymlicka, 1995: Chapter 5), and then assumes people's national affiliations to one set of traditions and national values, including language, religion, etc. What is ultimately problematical with this picture is the conception of culture that is being mobilized, in which the apparently neutral term actually turns out to be national-state based. Thus, a culture is conceived as a unitary and a bounded state entity, as the property of a particular national group, as distinct from the cultures of other groups, and as fixed and constant through time. This reinforces the notion that the authentic way of conducting one's life can only be assured through the national experience, that is, living within state-controlled and nationally defined and nationally delineated borders.

Taking this perspective, it seems to me that multicultural citizenship has more in common with assimilationist and homogeneous minds.

They share interpretative frameworks of diversity, namely in the way they similarly categorize attributes such as nationality, race, religion and community. Multiculturalists, to my knowledge, have never formulated a critical assessment regarding the way homogeneous cultural and national states categorize diversity dynamics. Intercultural citizenship's premise is that we cannot impose our diversity categories on others. This also involves putting into doubt the glue of most of the multicultural debates between ethnicity and nationality. Ethnicity is self-ascribed, flexible and cannot be imposed by those with the power to define diversity categories. Ethnicity, understood as self-identification, concerns the categories of ascription. Ethnic boundaries are also places of social interactions. The intercultural citizenship paradigm reacts against the process of political ethnicization of people and against considering ethnicity as a given notion in categorizing groups. This substantial criticism of the multicultural citizenship approach in the domains of ethnicity, nationalism and race is very close to what Brubaker calls 'groupism', in other words, 'the tendency to treat ethnic groups, nations and races as substantial entities to which interests and agency can be attributed' (2002: 164), or even 'solitarism' as referred to by Sen (2006: xii–xiii), criticizing this tendency to reduce people to singular, differentiated identity affiliations, to 'miniaturize' people into one dimension of their multiple identities. The summary of these arguments is clear. The transnational reality in which most people live today tells us that mostly birthplace and/or nationality do not determine public identities. To ask someone where he/she was born with the purpose of gaining an initial idea of what public identity he/she holds is not as self-evident as it was in the past. Several studies working on transnational and complex identities as an empirical category show us that transnationalism and people's growing mobility are currently pluralizing identities and the self-national and cultural adscriptions (Favell, 2014). This is now the rule, one that needs to be incorporated into the current diversity debate.

In this chapter I will provide reasons why I think that intercultural citizenship is a better approach for dealing with the complexity of our super-diverse societies, with transnational and multiple identities and cultural affiliations, with cosmopolitan and solidarity horizons. In section 1 I introduce the notion of methodological interculturalism, directly addressed to break the epistemological barriers left by methodological nationalism, of which multiculturalism is a by-product. This will allow me to discuss the links of intercultural citizenship with the new patterns of our societies: mainstreaming policies, transnationalism, super-diversity and the two new horizons of our diversity debate: cosmopolitanism and solidarity.

1. METHODOLOGICAL INTERCULTURALISM: BREAKING DOWN EPISTEMOLOGICAL BARRIERS[2]

I would like to briefly pursue a line of argumentation articulating what I consider is one of the key epistemological foundations of interculturalism. In spite of sharing with multiculturalism the recognition of the inevitability of diversity in modern cities, of opposing monoculturalist assimilation strategies, and that both seek equal treatment of difference (Meer et al., 2016: 9), there are some new trends in the diversity debate where multiculturalism clearly shows its limitations. These epistemological implications give interculturalism its proper place within the diversity debate. Let me call this dimension *methodological interculturalism.*

The premise is that the new diversity dynamics creates a need to discuss new conceptual maps. For this, we need to break down old conceptual barriers, which have been dominant these last decades, in large part produced by the multiculturalism narrative. Methodological interculturalism is a promising epistemological lens through which to look at new theoretical diversity-related paradigms. The premise is the assumption that diversity and difference is a fact that we need to incorporate into our public culture. It is a direct answer to the key question, what happens when the unit of analysis, the initial premise from which we argue about 'how to live together' is diversity itself rather than a supposed us/we/unity/majority/state/nation lens? What happens if we begin to formulate arguments taking diversity as the main vantage point? In this case, we need to assume that diversity is not only a fact but a culture that needs to be fostered by public institutions. This culture of diversity encompasses that differences should fundamentally be the object of affirmation and not negation, and that diversity needs to be separated from a national-based and ethnic-based (even racial-based) perception of identity. Methodological interculturalism also requests that it is through this diversity-lens that we must review mainstream public policies. In this framework, methodological interculturalism highlights

---

[2]This section is a re-edition (with some adjustments) of the article published in Zapata-Barrero, R. (2019) 'Methodological interculturalism: breaking down epistemological barriers around diversity management', *Ethnic and Racial Studies*, 42(3): 346–56.

the importance of contact between people, seen as the most appropriate way to drive integration (can integration and diversity accommodation be done without contact, by only distributing differentiated rights, as multiculturalism has defended for decades?).

Through methodological interculturalism, I want to give to interculturalism its proper foundation. It helps me to channel most of the emerging theoretical paradigms that have been put forward these past years, distinguishing the distinctive features and new dynamics of diversity and migration: transnationalism, super-diversity, cosmopolitanism and solidarity. As frameworks of analysis, all request, albeit from different angles, going beyond what has been popularized as methodological nationalism (Wimmer and Glick Schiller, 2003).

Methodological interculturalism is some sort of Copernican turn. We know that Bacon famously identified what he considered the main errors in the human attempt to gain knowledge. He called these errors 'idols', suggesting that these are ideas that are taken for granted, which influences the way we produce knowledge and explains why so many minds hold so many false ideas for long periods of time. These 'multicultural idols' have framed a great part of the past scholarly decade on diversity management, and are now being disputed through methodological interculturalism. Beyond the national narrative domination: the local turn; beyond ethnocentrism and group-based narrative hegemony: the return to the individual; beyond the immigrant/citizenship divide of the population narrative framework: the mainstreaming turn (see section 2).

The basis of methodological interculturalism turns these three parameters around, together with the epistemological assumptions that have governed these last decades of migration studies: Unity/Diversity and Majority/Minority nexus. It is a fact that in the post-M era we are entering, we cannot accept as a premise that those who define diversity do not include themselves within this category. If we want to take a step forward within the diversity debate, we simply cannot uncritically accept that diversity be used as a euphemism to perpetuate the us/others separation of societies.

Methodological interculturalism, then, plays a prominent role in legitimizing the new needed epistemology to deal with new diversity geography. It can cluster transnationalism, super-diversity, cosmopolitanism and solidarity debates on diversity today. This fact legitimizes its distinctive features as a policy paradigm today, since it helps us give answers to the diversity concerns that these theoretical paradigms invite us to challenge. But before briefly going into these theoretical frameworks, it is also important to insist that this new epistemology can only work if intercultural citizenship is consolidated as a mainstreaming policy.

2. INTERCULTURAL CITIZENSHIP AND MAINSTREAMING POLICIES: ELECTIVE AFFINITY[3]

The current context of an ideological crisis of the multicultural policy paradigm is certainly a contextual factor favouring the elective affinity[4] between interculturalism and mainstreaming, to the point that we can say today that mainstreaming is a distinctive feature of the intercultural citizenship philosophy. In fact, this interface provides intercultural citizenship with a powerful competitive policy tool, solving most of the policy makers' concerns with the multicultural citizenship approach. To strengthen this link, we could even speak about 'mainstreaming the intercultural citizenship policy paradigm' as a way to designate a public-policy philosophy that emphasizes both the importance of promoting communication, interpersonal diversity-related exchanges in all spheres of public life and basic structures of society, and of all the population contributing to the diversity dynamics, including nationals. The logical relationship between them is clear: mainstreaming is one of the core attributes of intercultural citizenship, and it can only be implemented when it targets everyone. In practical terms, this means that mainstreaming is the proper policy strategy to achieve intercultural citizenship.

At this stage of my rationale, it is probably difficult, and even adventurous, to say what factor(s) provoke the attraction of intercultural citizenship, but the fact is that we are in the presence of two policy trends that coincide in time and space, and even reinforce each other's legitimacy. That is, the interculturalism policy paradigm is justified because it has mainstreaming as its main strategy of implementation, and mainstreaming applied to migration-related diversity management leads naturally to interculturalism.

The elective affinity between mainstreaming and intercultural citizenship seems then to be self-evident. Mainstreaming policy directly breaks the background narrative framework that continuously reproduces the multi-

---

[3] This section summarizes the main arguments put forward in Zapata-Barrero, R. (2017b).

[4] Mid-eighteenth century (as elective attraction): originally a technical term for the preferential combination of chemical substances, it was widely used figuratively in the nineteenth century, notably by Goethe (in his novel *Elective Affinities*) and by Weber (in describing the correspondence between aspects of protestantism and capitalism). In its common use 'elective affinity' means 'A correspondence with, or feeling of sympathy or attraction towards, a particular idea, attitude, or person', English Oxford Living Dictionaries: @OxfordWords (www.en.oxforddictionaries.com/definition/elective_affinity).

cultural citizenship paradigm, differentiating migrants from citizens. In broadening the scope of the target public to one that encompasses all the resident population, we would probably need to leave aside the name of im/migration policy, and speak rather of intercultural citizenship as a mainstreaming policy.

In targeting the broad population and incorporating diversity concerns within the general public-policy focus, intercultural citizenship seeks to be incorporated into policy-making at all city levels and in all departments. The final goal is to create public services that are attuned to the needs of the whole population, regardless of their background. It has also been recently and rightly defined as an effort to reach people with a migrant background through needs-based social programming and policies that also target the general population (Collet and Petrovic, 2014: 2).

Intercultural citizenship provides answers for local concerns and this city-based origin is probably one of the factors justifying the adoption of mainstreaming policy strategies. There are multiple factors explaining the mainstreaming move of diversity policies (Scholten and Van Breugel, 2017); I will concentrate on the declining political support for multicultural policies in most European cities (Lewis, 2014; Taras, 2012).

Mainstreaming's conceptual core refers to incorporating the needs and issues of a particular service into a general area or system and into all aspects of an organization's policy and practice (Scholten and Van Breugel, 2017: Chapter 1). Applied to diversity management, it essentially means an overhaul of how we have been doing things in the past and the inclusion of a new policy perspective in all that we do. It is here that interculturalism meets the mainstreaming debate, since its principal aim is the promote contact zones among different people (whatever their origin, including nationals) in diversity contexts (Zapata-Barrero, 2016b: 56). And the dominant policy paradigm of diversity management of 'how we have been doing things in the past' has certainly been multicultural citizenship.

It is in this sense that we may say that mainstreaming intercultural citizenship becomes a new policy paradigm, since it frames the focus of several public policies, and even all basic pillars of the structure of local societies, both through public discourse that explicitly incorporates intercultural citizenship priorities, and through mainstreaming governance, which involves coordinating a range of public and civil society actors participating in policy-making, either horizontally (by involving other policy departments at the same level) or vertically (by distributing responsibilities across multiple territorial levels of government).

As a policy paradigm, mainstreaming intercultural citizenship refers, then, to the adaptations of general policies that incorporate intercultural priorities. This policy adaptation is designed to better serve the diverse populations that benefit from public policies by responding to their specific needs rather than preconceptions of the needs of national cultural groups. If we take, for instance, the categories indexing intercultural cities,[5] we see that it has both an integral dimension and an expansive scope in all the main spheres of society (from media to governance, public spheres, mediators and other city realms). Intercultural citizenship features this mainstreaming approach in the sense that it does not legitimize any specific policy justified in ethnic and whatever cultural-group terms. Intercultural citizenship as a mainstreaming policy is, then, a departure from ethnicity-based diversity paradigms, which are also blind to the internal diversity and stratification of ethnic groups and fail to address the key challenge of integration of second generations through social mobility and full citizenship.

3. TRANSNATIONAL CITIZENSHIP AND INTERCULTURAL CITIZENSHIP: OVERLAPPING AFFINITIES[6]

The fact that migratory dynamics provoke new ways of thinking about national identities and territorial settlement has been at the core of the transnational field of research, and, from the very beginning, was associated with the globalization of cross-state human mobility.[7] If strict assimilation were the norm, diversity would be considered as a transitory process rather than a new permanent feature of our societies.

The seminal idea that I would like to articulate here is that transnational citizenship necessarily contains intercultural practice, and intercultural citizenship is a way to understand transnational behaviour. This follows my main argument: the growing importance of people with multiple national identity affiliations (the basis of transnational citizenship) is a favourable context for promoting contact between diverse people, including national citizens

---

[5] See www.coe.int/en/web/interculturalcities/about-the-index.

[6] This section summarizes the main arguments put forward in Zapata-Barrero, R. (2018b).

[7] Most of the literature on transnationalism will be mentioned in the text. But for this matter, see some of the latest review literature and compelling works on transnationalism: Faist et al., 2013; Mügge, 2016; Portes and Fernández-Kelly, 2015.

(the basis of intercultural citizenship). In order to enter this empirical discussion, I will follow a rationale in two steps: first, I will show how transnational citizenship can be understood as a new context that helps us to illustrate our complex diverse societies; and second, that this transnational context is the appropriate condition that can help the widespread expansion of the intercultural citizenship policy paradigm, given that interculturalism and transnationalism present some 'overlapping affinities'. By this last notion, and in the absence of a better one, I want to emphasize that there is not just a juxtaposition between transnational citizenship and intercultural citizenship, but that each one necessarily contains the other in order to define its main conceptual dimensions and functional characteristics.

Transnational citizens are at least bilingual, move easily between different cultures, frequently maintain homes in two countries, and also pursue economic, political and cultural interests with both their countries, and even decide to run their business in their home countries, as transnational entrepreneurs, as has been recently signalled as an emerging global social pattern (Zapata-Barrero and Rezaei, 2019). These complex identities are becoming more and more the norm in our diverse societies, in part also determined by readily accesible communication platforms, such as Skype, WhatsApp and other social technological means, including low-cost travel.

Transnationalism is therefore a new scenario that perfectly defines one of the main features of our diverse societies, and creates a social space in which many people with multiple national-identies can relate to one another. The exception to this pattern is the idealistic view of national citizens, who still think of their country as though it were a territorial reality separated from the category of diversity. What has now been made more and more apparent is that 'the notion of primary loyalty to one place is therefore misleading: it was an icon of old-style nationalism that has little relevance for migrants in a mobile world' (Castles, 2016: 290). The fact that transnational contexts in our societies are becoming the norm also means there is a growing favourable context for implementing intercultural citizenship.

Theoretically speaking, I am not formulating a direct relationship between transnational citizenship, complex diversity settings and intercultural practices (i.e. suggesting that all transnational citizens are intercultural citizens), but rather I suggest that there is a predisposition if, and only if, there is a policy that promotes contact. Diversity-related contact is not self-evident. The permanent premise of intercultural citizenship is that contact between people can help to establish positive feelings when they take place in a cooperative environment among equals (this has been examined in detail in Chapter 1). In other words, the transnational context by itself does not necessarily promote contact between, let's say, a Chinese and a Moroccan individual. But if there is a policy that looks for common bonds and interests between these two people, and uses this to push them into common views and projects, it is probable that due to their familiarity with the migrant experience and from living within their own transnational mind, these individuals would have a tendency to be increasingly intercultural. It is here that we can justify intercultural citizenship as a strategy to promote positive contact among people with different backgrounds, but here lie many common bonds and interests that we simply need to identify through an intercultural policy lens.

If we look at transcultural activities in residence countries, such as the celebration of a national day, religious-cultural activities that bond people with their national and cultural home identities, we can say that these practices are transnational in the sense that people combine national origin and current national residence in the same space in which they live. This can be an example of transnational nationalism or of the de-territorialization of the national identity.[8] These activities are, by themselves, intercultural, since they promote encounters between people from different backgrounds in public spaces, the main space of intercultural practices (see Chapter 8).

For us, these transnational activities, and the transnational character of a person entering into these practices, have some overlapping affinities with interculturalism in two ways. First, it involves internal personal contact with at least two national identities, generally speaking, home and receiving/host national identities. This means that transnational people are like this precisely because they have already entered into an intrapersonal dialogue with two national identities. Second, this bi-national identity gives rise to determinate practices under the form of maintaining regular contact with relatives and friends, and the different social spaces left behind during the migratory process, or with the nationality of their own families, if they are second generation. This again involves intercultural citizenship.

---

[8]The idea of 'deterritorialisation' has been from the very beginning a premise of the transnational literature; see, for instance, Basch et al. (1994). It has also been re-stated by R. Kastoryano, when she defines transnational nationalism as a type of nationalism without territory. She has recently emphasized that: 'The transnational nation fits within the global space which does not *reflect* but *produces* an identity and generates a mode of participation beyond borders, as can be seen in the involvement of actors in strengthening transnational solidarities' (Kastoryano, 2016: 55; Translation from French by the Author).

The fact that people with more than one national identity are more prone to have social ties is at the core of most recent empirical research. For instance, the work of Ramarajan (2014) shows how multiple identities shape people's actions. Multiple identities foster intrapersonal identity networks, in which the nodes of the network are identities (which can vary in aspects such as number and importance) and in which the ties of the network are relationships, such as those of conflict, enhancement and integration. Scholars can then examine the various structures or patterns of relationships among multiple identities. Drawing on ideas of associative networks in psychology, as well as on social networks in sociology, Ramarajan (2014) makes the case for a network conceptualization of multiple identities. This provides us with ways of understanding how identities operate as entire systems in which parts (identities) are connected (via relationships) to form a whole (a network of identities). Further research coming from business studies also shows how multiple identities shape important outcomes in organizations, such as intergroup tolerance (Roccas and Brewer, 2002). Multiple intrapersonal identities also seem to influence interpersonal and intergroup relationships, although this research also suggests the potential for both positive and negative consequences. In the same line of analysis, some other empirical studies show that multiple identities are positively related to intergroup cooperation (Brewer and Pierce, 2005; Richter et al., 2006). Roccas and Brewer (2002) have also predicted that social identity complexity is related to personal value priorities and to tolerance of out-group people. One thing that has not been previously taken into account in trying to explain these variations in the perceptions of others is the way in which the perceiver represents his or her own multiple category identities. For instance, how a person who is both white and Christian responds to another individual who is black and Christian may well depend on how the perceiver self-defines his or her own racial and religious identities.

This also confirms one of the key features of interculturalism in contrast to multiculturalism. The latter focuses its policies on preserving differences and protecting them through rights. In contrast, intercultural citizenship focuses on commonalties (in the previous example, the fact that both are Christians facilitates communication between a black and a white person, for instance). The premise is obvious: you can only promote contact if there is something in common between two people in their multiple identities. This commonality does not necessarily need to be a category of diversity, as I have shown in the above example, but a common interest (cooking, for instance) or work (both are doctors and interested in a concrete challenging disease, for instance). This is also the basis of the bridging principle driving intercultural citizenship. For these studies, understanding the structure of multiple social identities is important because representations of one's in-groups have an effect not only on the concept of self, but also on the nature of the relationships between the self and others (Roccas and Brewer, 2002: 88). Social identity complexity is based upon chronic awareness of cross-categorization in one's own social-group memberships and in those of others. A simple social identity is likely to be accompanied by the perception that any individual who is an out-group member on one dimension is also an out-group member on all others. In sum, social psychology studies have shown that both cognitive and motivational factors lead us to predict that complex social identities will be associated with increased tolerance and positivity towards out-groups in general. Here, again, the connection between transnational citizenship and intercultural citizenship is very clear.

To summarize: the first and foremost reason why transnationalism deserves attention today is its sheer growth in recent years. Its existence is highly relevant to some recent works on cities (Glick Schiller, 2011), an area where interculturalism also develops its main policies (see Chapter 2). Thus, a transnational framework gives policy makers a new lens through which to develop innovative public intercultural citizenship programmes inside their local communities and even beyond, promoting intercultural relations with the home cities of their proper transnational inhabitants.

4. NEW HORIZONS: COSMOPOLITANISM AND SOLIDARITY

Through migration studies, cosmopolitanism develops a sense of awareness to live in a complex diverse society, and that oneself is just one part of this diverse geography. The initial premise is that the growth of human mobility and the consequent encounters with difference inevitably lead people to step beyond the national boundaries to establish shared bonds (Beck and Sznaider, 2006; Glick Schiller and Irving, 2017). The application of cosmopolitanism to migration studies has been basically done through the notion of a community of strangers (Derrida, Henig, Kristeva), or the idea that the majority do not feel they are from the same community but quite the contrary – everyone feels like a stranger and different, and then this common feeling of difference is what can unite us and lead us to develop feelings of hospitality and welcomeness. Epistemologically, this also means that there is not an 'us' in this cosmopolitan word, because everyone is the 'other'.

The shared argument is that all human beings are or can and should be citizens in a single community (whatever size we apply). Every cosmopolitan argues for community-building (a cosmopolitan representative of interculturalism is probably Cantle, 2012).

Formulating the view in negative terms, the cosmopolitan position rejects exclusive attachments to a particular national culture. The epistemological consequence here is that cosmopolitanism cannot be understood today without this encouragement of cultural diversity and intercultural encounters. In a cosmopolitan community individuals from different places (e.g. nation-states) and cultural/religious beliefs enter in relationships of mutual respect. Related to identity and culture it also means that even if I see myself as different from others, this does not necessarily mean we must have separate lives because we have nothing in common. This again means that we should incorporate diversity as a public culture, and then place diversity-recognition as the brand of the new society. In this view, cosmopolitanism is a way to say that there is no rational ground for curtailing the cultural freedoms (of language, religion and customs) in the name of a so-called majoritarian nation/church, or cultural dominant ideology. Cosmopolitanism also assumes culture is a fluid concept, elastic, open-ended, not atemporally fixed, which is also the basis of methodological interculturalism.

It follows that there are some affinities between cosmopolitan and intercultural citizenship. Not only because both focus on what is common within difference but also both prioritize human rights, and refuse to interpret diversity from just one national identity affiliation or link to a culture/territory. Within this framework, methodological interculturalism tells us that fostering contact is a strategy to build a cosmopolitan community.

The fact that people relate to each other, in different place-settings, for different shared purposes, indicates that they develop a cosmopolitan culture: that is, that they understand other people can have different views about ways of living, religion and language, and that they recognize and respect them just as they too would like their own views to be respected and recognized by others. The first principle of interculturalism can also be applied to cosmopolitan culture: diversity-recognition and self-recognition are not separate from but also belong to the diversity category. It is this open mindedness that constitutes a cosmopolitan culture. If diverse people live together but just one does not respect diversity, then a cosmopolitan problem may arise under the form of racism, xenophobia or whatever diversity-adverse behaviour. From an intercultural point of view, a cosmopolitan culture involves, then, that it is possible to recognize ourselves in our interactions with others.

Vertovec and Cohen (2002) rightly synthetize this vision suggesting that cosmopolitanism simultaneously (a) transcends the seemingly exhausted nation-state model, (b) is able to mediate actions and ideals oriented to the universal and the particular, the global and the local, (c) is culturally anti-essentialist, and (d) is capable of representing variously complex repertoires of allegiance, identity and interest. In these ways, cosmopolitanism seems to offer a mode of managing cultural and political multiplicities. In this sense, we can say that intercultural people have a cosmopolitan mindset.

The concept of solidarity has recently been incorporated into the migration research agenda through two distinct avenues. First, in refugee studies, solidarity has been placed at the centre of the counter-argument against the state-based narrative on security. Solidarity is the main city narrative, also expressed through welcoming cities, along similar lines to non-governmental organizations (NGOs) and citizens expressing their commitment to the destiny of forced migrants. In normative terms, political realism is competing with a much more humanitarian approach.

Second, in diversity studies, solidarity has been connected to what Banting and Kymlicka (2006) label as the corroding effect of the multicultural project; that is, the fact that multicultural policies' unintended effects have been lack of trust, solidarity and social capital. Here lies the place of solidarity as one of the cornerstones of welfare states. Solidarity refers to the practice of sharing material/immaterial resources on the basis of a sense of belonging and group loyalty. Traditionally the concept has assumed a certain sense of community, which is the basis of action. If this basis is humanity, solidarity can be expressed to all human beings. But generally, as a principle driving policy, solidarity has not been linked to cosmopolitanism. Inverting the argument, non-solidarity situations reveal a certain failure of community cohesion and shared values.

Behind these statements there is a sense of belonging, but also some emotional ties (empathy) to the situation of disadvantage of certain people who require external help. In this scenario, the increasingly diverse social fabric has come into conflict with the traditional idea that solidarity is necessarily embedded in an imagined homogeneous national community (Banting and Kymlicka, 2015). Today, solidarity among cultural equals versus solidarity among those who are culturally different becomes a framework of reflection. One common trend of this theoretical paradigm is that it basically has a normative meaning, and it is linked, again, with a determinate idea of justice. In whatever situation requiring the application of the solidarity principle, a determinate unjust equality-related situation arises.

When we link it to migration-related diversity management a mirror effect takes place, and we see how traditionally solidarity has been embedded with a determined view of a social community with a shared (national) history and shared (national) norms and values. Today, in super-diverse and transnational societies, solidarity has real difficulties in remaining within this national-state paradigm. Hence, this need to reboot the traditional view of solidarity is claiming, again, methodological interculturalism. Solidarity incorporating super-diverse and transnational realities has not been theorized enough, but we can place as a premise the need for contact and intercultural encounters as a policy strategy to foster solidarity in diverse societies.

PART II

FOUNDATIONS OF INTERCULTURAL CITIZENSHIP

5

CONCEPTUALIZING INTERCULTURAL CITIZENSHIP'S DIVERSITY-LINKAGE THEORY

INTRODUCTION: CONTACT THEORY, THE BASIS OF INTERCULTURAL CITIZENSHIP

Intercultural citizenship calls for proximity, connectivity and diversity-related activities. It also calls for shared spaces, common public culture and mutual diversity-recognition. It points to the common humanity that emerges from diversity-related exchanges, rather than fixing its interest on the differences of ethnicity, race, religion, language, etc. Intercultural citizenship can be viewed descriptively and normatively. The descriptive meaning conceptualizes a diversity-linkage theory. It understands contact as being the basis for diversity-related exchange and diversity-related learning, the driving of a socialization process for incorporating diversity as a public culture into the citizenry. The normative meaning deals with the different strands of intercultural citizenship, or the different ways to justify why a policy intervention promoting diversity-contacts is necessary and what theoretical frameworks can shape this policy. In this chapter I will concentrate on the descriptive meaning, and go to the normative sense in the next chapter.

We now enter the domain of actual human relations in a diverse environment. These entail a range of contacts from fleeting to sustained exchanges, linkages and communications. It concerns the micro-sociological level, which is consubstantial with intercultural citizenship. It is common to refer to Allport's contact hypothesis, but we shall do so without ignoring its often neglected premise; namely, and in his own words: 'it has sometimes been held that merely by assembling people without regard for race, colour, religion, or national origin, we can thereby destroy stereotypes and develop friendly attitudes. The case is not so simple' (Allport, 1954: 261). And he immediately warns that 'the effects of contact obviously depend upon the kind of association that occurs, and upon the kinds of persons who are involved' (1954: 261–2). This starting point is necessary but we need to go beyond, since, as Zuma (2014: 44) reminds us, 'contact theory is fundamentally a prejudice and not an interracial relations/interethnic theory'. The multiple uses of the contact hypothesis beyond its original circle are, however, what have controlled the debate since then. We should also emphasize that one deficit of this original contact theory is that it does not necessarily have the transformative dimension we give to diversity-contact. In this sense, intercultural citizenship promotes contact not only to reduce prejudice and foster mutual knowledge, but for promoting a new public culture which understands diversity itself as a culture, or what I call a public culture of diversity. I will take all these premises as a starting point for theorizing diversity-contact of the intercultural citizenship paradigm.

Taking on these previous warnings from Allport, Forbes (1997: 20) reminds us that Allport goes through a variety of meanings of contact, from causal contact to true acquaintance. Causal contact, superficial encounters, proximity without familiarity may even increase prejudice rather than dispelling it. So not all contact is positive. True acquaintance, he says, lessens prejudices. As Allport pointed out, there is a need to meet certain conditions. The four conditions under which prejudices can be reduced are clearly stated in one seminal sentence:

> Prejudice (unless deeply rooted in the character structure of the individual) may be reduced by equal status contact between majority and minority groups in the pursuit of common goals. The effect is greatly enhanced if this contact is sanctioned by institutional support (i.e., by law, custom or local atmosphere), and provided it is of a sort that leads to the perception of common interests and common humanity between members of the two groups. (1954: 281)

Before continuing, let me provide a reminder of what the bases of the contact hypothesis are. The premise of Allport's theory states that under conditions of equality and power sharing, inter-personal contact is one of the most effective ways to reduce prejudice. We can extend this hypothesis to accept that this also assumes recognizing diversity and that oneself belongs to this diversity. If a person has the opportunity to communicate with others, he or she will also be able to understand and appreciate different points of views involving his or her way of life, and may also be open to changing his or her views as a direct outcome of contact. As a result of new appreciation and understanding, prejudice should diminish. Issues of stereotyping, prejudice and discrimination commonly occur between people who are in a competitive logic. This is why prejudices not only have an identity component, but also a social class one (Pettigrew and Tropp, 2013). Fainstein (2005: 13), for instance, affirms that the relationship between diversity and tolerance is not clear. Sometimes exposure to 'the other' evokes greater understanding, but if lifestyles are too incompatible, it only heightens prejudice. Allport's proposal was that properly managed contact should reduce these problems and lead to better interactions. Some of the Allport's criteria can be adapted to intercultural citizenship focus, as follows:

- *Equal status within difference.* People must engage equally in the relationship. This means that people should have similar backgrounds, qualities and characteristics. Differences in education, wealth, skills or experiences may perhaps reduce the possibilities of positive contact when this involves interpersonal relations between people from different nations, languages, religions and cultures. Let me give an example. The contact between a person of Tunisian origin may be easier with another person from another nationality/culture/religion, let's say Colombian, if this occurs among people from the same level of education/social class, age and gender, for instance. Or to put it in another away, contact between a lower-class Pakistani person with an upper-class Argentinian will most probably not be positive since there is no common denominator such as a similar social background.
- *Common goals' interdependence.* People must work on a problem/task and share this as a common project. There is awareness that this project's goal can only be attained if people work together by pooling their efforts and resources.
- *Cooperation.* People must work together in a non-competitive atmosphere, without feeling they are losing something or that their interest will not be reached. We can perfectly see that this condition is key for the others. That is, the examples given before on equal status can only work if there is a cooperative environment. The same social class with different nationalities can be competitive and then can shape an unfavourable environment for positive contact.
- *Support of authorities, law or customs.* People acknowledge that some authorities support contact and even promote interactions between people from diverse backgrounds. This contact is then done in a friendly, helpful atmosphere, since there is awareness that it is institutionally or traditionally endorsed.

This prejudice-reduction and mutual knowledge-promotion through interpersonal contact is the basis of intercultural citizenship, when applied in local diversity settings. Behind this contact hypothesis there is obviously the assumption that prejudices, stereotypes and rumours are among the main factors hindering contact, and that there is always a supposition that prejudices are based on misunderstandings and are a likely direct result of generalizations and oversimplifications made about others based on incomplete or mistaken information. From intercultural citizenship's perspective, the basic rationale, then, is that this negative factor for contact may be reduced as people learn more about others. This change in beliefs and willingness to change one's mind is also crucial as a premise for positive contact. This is what diversity-recognition involves at the individual level: contact can be an antidote against fundamentalist and extreme ideologies that tend to want to impose people's view on others and see other views in competitive terms.

Apart from the specific encounters, which were arranged to tackle these specific problems, contact theory has demonstrated how to improve intercultural understanding through 'everyday' and unplanned encounters. These encounters enable stereotypes and preconceptions to be directly challenged and the fear of 'others' to be reduced. We then assume that the immediate context of living plays a pivotal role for building perception on diversity (Schönwälder et al., 2016). However, perhaps the most significant evidence of the success of this approach has been demonstrated by a meta-analysis conducted by Pettigrew and Tropp (2006) across many countries and which concluded that 'the present article presents a meta-analytic test of intergroup contact theory. With 713 independent samples from 515 studies, the meta-analysis finds that intergroup contact typically reduces intergroup prejudice' (2006: 751).

Taking into account these premises, I will begin in section 1 to overview the relational sociologist's contributions, mapping a variety of contacts. I will then go to section 2 from the angle of what intercultural citizenship promotes in the way of relations. This will help me to summarize the main relational categories through what I will call a 'diversity-linkage theory' informing intercultural citizenship.

1. RELATIONAL SOCIOLOGISTS' CONTRIBUTIONS ON THE VARIETY OF CONTACTS

Following Allport's warnings, the variety of contexts where contact takes place is also to be considered in any exploratory theory of diversity-contact for intercultural citizenship. In other words, situational contacts are what matters for intercultural citizenship. There can be residential, occupational and social contacts. Again, the literature often stresses that simply living or working side by side is less important than the forms of communication that may result from proximity. Some influential studies even problematize the causal mechanism, which has been taken for granted since then. Pettigrew (1998), for instance, stresses the failure to establish the causal sequence of contact. He states that the relation may be circular, indeed, in the context of whether contact reduces prejudice or prejudice reduces contact.

Diversity-contact can in fact be a complex web of diverse relations. Bynner (2016: 27–8), for instance, frames intercultural contact at the local level and proposes three forms depending on how the contact is focused: Deliberative (involves dialogue and debate between individuals or representatives of local people in relation to addressing problems and issues within the neighbourhood), Transformative (based on a shared interest, leisure activity or learning experiences, it usually expands initial perspectives), and Neighbour (involving face-to-face contact between individuals and families who are immediate neighbours and are known to one another). Contact also tends to be informal, focused on a small geographical area, and varies in intensity, intimacy and duration. These forms of social interaction are usually based on sharing a common space such as a building, a block within a street of adjoining buildings, or other micro-spaces. Some other scholars also offer us stimulating analytical distinctions. Lofland (1998: 51ff), for instance, distinguishes different types of person-to-person connections. (a) Fleeting relationships are the most representative in public spaces, occurring between persons who are personally unknown to one another (among strangers basically). They have a very brief duration, and spoken exchanges can occur or not. (b) Routinized relationships are a secondary relatively standardized character of the contact (the relation as learned routine). Examples come from bus drivers, shopping relations, etc. (c) Quasi-primary relationships are brief encounters (lasting from a few minutes to several hours) between strangers or between those who are categorically known to one another (a friendly chat between dog owners, exchange of criticism between two pedestrians, more extended conversation between seat mates on buses or airplanes, users of laundromats, etc.). Finally, (d) intimate-secondary relationships are relatively long-standing, and involve more sharing of personal information, more socializing and more diffusion of purpose, for example a personal on-going and recurring link with the same customer, or with some neighbourhoods, hairdressers, etc.

Another set of distinctions come from the interactionist Blumer (1969), when he differentiates between 'symbolic' and 'non-symbolic' interaction. In his summarizing statement of 'The Methodological Position of Symbolic Interactionism', he reiterated that classic distinction in these terms:

non-symbolic interaction takes place when a person responds directly to the action of another without interpreting that action; symbolic interaction involves interpretation of the action. Non-symbolic interaction is most readily apparent in reflex responses, as in the case of a boxer who automatically raises his arm to parry a blow [...] In their association human beings engage plentifully in non-symbolic interaction as they respond immediately and unreflectively to each other's bodily movements, expressions, and tones of voice, but their characteristic mode of interaction is on the symbolic level, as they seek to understand the meaning of each other's actions. (Blumer, 1969: 8–9)

Let me also quote a last relational sociologist: the classical Simmel and his work on the construction of the stranger, in which he introduces us to what he calls 'different forms of socialization' (Simmel, 2009[1908]). His focus is on the sensitive experiences people may have. The stranger is a social form and it is categorized as the other as far as he or she does not belong to a social circle. The stranger can generate sensitive experiences such as familiarity or estrangement, acceptance or rejection. Within this rationale, Simmel introduces a suggestive notion of 'sensitive proximity' in shared spaces. His premise is that in moments of spatial proximity between people, a sensitive grasp of the other may be experienced via the senses. This notion refers to a concrete relation between the body (sensitivity) and space (proximity). For Simmel, this is why through interaction we not only give meaning to the gestures and overall appearance of others (garments, movements, poise), but we also feel them. This creates emotions and effects that can range from pleasure to disgust, from attraction to repulsion. Simmel then states that

> towards the spatially near, with whom one is reciprocally involved in the most varied situations and moods without the possibility of foresight and choice, there tends to be then definite feelings so that this proximity can be the foundation of the most exuberant joy as well as the most unbearable coercion. (Simmel 2009[1908]: 569)

Following this approach, we can develop notions such as sensitive boundaries, sensitive expectations and exchanges. Sensitive impacts may then be meaningful to understand the notion of diversity-contact behind intercultural citizenship.

In fact, we could pursue this first mapping exercise quoting many classical sociologists, since sociology's seminal interest has always been to understand the variety of relations there are among people. All these analytical distinctions could be perfectly applied to inter-personal diversity-contacts taking place in public, in contrast to private forms. The final form of intercultural citizenship is public, defined here as involving face-to-face contact between individuals who are often strangers to each other and who share the same public space. Contacts may involve verbal and non-verbal communication, and make use of body language, and awareness or avoidance of others in public space (we will go into this dimension when speaking about public spaces in Chapter 7).

2. INTERCULTURAL CITIZENSHIP AS A STRATEGY OF BUILDING RELATIONSHIPS

Intercultural citizenship is the outcome of a strategy of building relationships within diversity settings. Given these preliminary clarifications and possibilities of contacts, what are those that may help us to better foster intercultural citizenship? Contact can be very different if it is understood as dialogue or communication, sporadic encounter, interaction, inter-dependency or solidarity. Each type of contact may influence the way the socializing and learning process of intercultural citizenship proceeds in fostering a culture of diversity. The premise is the empirical evidence that the composition of the population in a particular area determines the likehood of coming into contact with others in everyday life (Schönwälder et al., 2016).

It is also important from the beginning to associate contact with conflict since they may produce different social action theories. We may first distinguish between the reactive and the preventive dimensions of intercultural citizenship in relation to diversity-related conflicts. 'Conflict zones' are defined here in a broad sense. They mean not only that there are different views that cannot be realized at the same time, and are then the result of a competitive logic of action, but also any manifestations of diversity-adversity taking place in society and that may influence the way contact between people may take place. Here, I consider 'conflict zones' as, for instance, any discriminatory practices, unequal and unbalanced power relations, racist and xenophobic attitudes. These modalities of power shape the way diversity is organized in particular places, spatializing the politics of diversification (Ye, 2017). All these reactive social practices against diversity contain the semantic of conflict I am using here. These conflict zones are the main areas of intercultural citizenship, which builds its strategies as a policy that has the purpose of transforming what was initially considered as a conflictive zone into a contact zone. This reactive-based approach of intercultural citizenship needs to be balanced with a much more preventive-based approach, where intercultural citizenship is seen as a strategy not for conflict-resolution but rather for preventing conflict-production by means of fostering positive outcomes produced through contact.

In both approaches, we need to identify the drivers that may facilitate positive contact and those that may precisely prevent this contact. As stated above, intercultural citizenship has its core foundation in Allport's contact hypothesis. Thus, we will take this theory as a premise to adapt more of its arguments to the intercultural citizenship approach. But before going to the drivers that may facilitate intercultural contact and those that may prevent it, let me stress that this contact theory cannot be detached from the fact that diversity settings primarily emerge on a local scale as a concrete and significant personal experience. It is at this level that an empirically based understanding can be advanced (Boccagni, 2015: 31). Urban diversity calls for proximity settings (workplace, schools, markets, streets and neighbourhood). Being placed in a post-M era and working with an expansive view of diversity, intercultural citizenship needs to also broaden the scope of contact and include criteria of social class, legal status, gender, age, and other markers of significant differentiation that may affect the way contact can produce positive or negative outcomes. This intersectionality needs to be incorporated in any theorization of contact informing intercultural citizenship. This involves that people cannot be fixed without checking its self-perception, and 'sensitive proximity' in Simmel's terms. It is rather how people self-identify and symbolically, in Blumer's terms, feel contact that drives intercultural citizenship. This potential of contact in cities must also be broadened: it is not only in public sectors, but rather in public spaces, which comprise institutional and non-institutional spaces. For instance, the potential of contact promotion in cafés, markets, gardens, public transport, etc. (Valentine, 2015) may help us to see how encounters may happen among people from different categories of diversity, or maybe a combination of them.

As diversity-linkage theory is one of the foundations of intercultural citizenship, it needs to be theorized following this focus, since we cannot assume a one-dimensional view of contact or that all contacts can have the same effect. Contacts can be practised in formal and informal settings, in many different public spaces, with many purposes and expectations; contact can be spontaneous, planned and meditated; it can take seconds, minutes, hours and even days. They can be reiterative or just one time. All these variations of contact, in time, space, intensity and grades, may have different outcomes. An appropriated theory of diversity-linkage informing intercultural citizenship needs to give answers to these variations and multi-faceted types of contact.

The fact that I have chosen the descriptive concept of contact is related to this effort to examine contact in gradual terms and define it following a multi-sited approach. This way I prefer this 'neutral' term of contact to the most popularized intercultural dialogue, which implies that there is some degree of negotiation between the two parts, which is not the case for contact. This is also evidence of how the intercultural dialogue narrative is anchored to its conflict-based origin. Dialogue is a strategy for negotiating in a conflictive context where the two approaches cannot be implemented at the same time. This irreconcilability of viewpoints within a competitive logic of action is what defines a situation as conflictive. 'Intercultural dialogue' comes from international relations, and it implies a strategy to solve ethnic conflicts at the global sphere. Intercultural dialogue involves, then, some sort of cultural *modus vivendi,* which is absent from the more 'neutral' concept of contact. Seeing intercultural citizenship as if it were a cultural identity negotiation needs to be rejected if we want to take seriously the intercultural citizenship focus. Indeed, intercultural citizenship promotes contact, but not with the purpose of offering some forum of negotiations among people in relation to their differentiations.

If we want to map a typology of diversity-contact as it is viewed by the intercultural citizenship approach we need a social action and a contextual approach of contact. The basic idea is then to reappraise the action theory of contact by also incorporating diversity, since the contact that interests us to theorize is not to be understood as 'sameness' but about people who feel they have some grounded differentiations (hence the 'diversity-related' notion that has helped me to write contact in its adjective form since the beginning). 'Contact' is an action-driven concept. The social action approach follows the Weberian definition (1978: 4) that says that 'an action is "social" if the acting individual takes account of the behaviour of others and is thereby oriented in its course'. The theory of social action entailed in this contact approach accepts and assumes that people vary in their actions according to social contexts and how it will affect other people; when a potential reaction is not desirable, the action is modified accordingly. This transformative dimension of contact is paramount for the intercultural citizenship paradigm. It is probably at this point, as I have already stressed, that the diversity-contact theory informing intercultural citizenship adds some new dimensions to Allport's original theory. If intercultural citizenship is a learning and socializing process, then contact must have as a final short-term purpose to provide understanding and knowledge to people so that they acquire a culture of diversity and can strengthen their diversity-recognition.

We may differentiate how strong the contact is in terms of time/frequency and also in terms of commitments. We may assume frequency is important in terms of strengthening the learning and socializing objectives of intercultural citizenship, and that time frame is also important. A contact that lasts five hours or days is not the same as a contact that lasts only a few seconds or minutes.

If the contact does not have any explicit interest for people we can call this a *diversity-encounter*. If this contact does not involve joint-action and a common interest, then the contact becomes an encounter, a social relation, lacking formality and personal interest. This encounter is often a simple socio-spatial coincidence, in the market or public transport for instance. If the contact is done for a common interest, then we can label this contact *diversity-interdependency*. In this case this joint-action pursues not only a common goal and interest, but there is common awareness that only by acting together is there more opportunity to reach the desired common goal. Then this shared goal becomes a distinctive feature of the contact, and we can speak about inter-dependency or inter-connected action. If the contact pursues shared interests and there is an awareness that by pursuing a joint-action the interest will be better reached than by pursuing it alone, then we may name this contact *diversity-interaction*. Usual examples of this are the several local projects for fostering a culture of diversity through common cultural practices and participation, cooking exchanges, sports and leisure, as well as other joint-actions. Finally, we may also include solidarity actions that are driven by the selfless commitment to others. This *diversity-solidarity* also involves that one engages in contact with another person with a differentiated feature (nationality, culture, religion, etc.) seeking to pursue the interest of the other person. Or to put it in another way, the interest of a solidarity action is to pursue the interest of another person, who we may represent as not having enough resources and skills to be able to reach it by themselves.

These four types of contacts can also be conventional or unconventional. A conventional inter-personal contact is one that takes place within an institutional framework where activities are delimited by a set of publicly recognized and accepted rules. An unconventional inter-personal contact is one that takes place in a much more open-ended atmosphere, where social routines and conventions are much more flexible, and in any case, they are not normatively delimited. A last categorization, and probably a classical one but that may be useful for intercultural citizenship, is that each diversity-contact can be formal or informal. An encounter in a market can be formal between two people: for instance, one Moroccan fruit seller and an elderly woman who is a national buying oranges. It can also take an informal shape, when the relation happens at a playground or on public transport, or while waiting for children in school and in the doctor's waiting room. Finally, another analytical distinction we may use for differentiating types of contacts that are informing intercultural citizenship is between public and private settings. We will have more opportunities to go into the public settings in Chapter 7, but now, for this line of analysis, we can say that the dividing line is how open or closed the realm is where the contact takes place. Clearly, a school, a theatre and a workplace are private spaces of contact. The market, the street, the playground are public spaces.

3. SUMMARY: INTERCULTURAL CITIZENSHIP'S PEOPLE LINKAGE THEORY

In describing the four types of contact that may influence the learning and socialization process of intercultural citizenship, whether they are conventional or unconventional, formal or informal, public or private, we have also assumed that there is always a cognitive and intentional component. This is important since this entails in its turn a certain diversity-recognition predisposition, which is, as it has been stated from the very beginning, the main condition of intercultural citizenship. This cognitive component means first of all awareness of being in this diversity environment, and the intentional one entails that there is a certain degree of interest-seeking that motivates people to be in contact. In fact, we may also label this diversity-contact conceptualization as a 'people linkage theory', in the sense that we emphasize the motivations and interests people may have to be connected to each other when they are aware that there is a certain differentiation category among them. In both cases, it is also striking to signal that these contacts (say linkages) can also happen if the structure of action is done autonomously, without any compulsory imposition forcing people to act in a determinate way. The policy followed by the intercultural citizenship paradigm is not a regulatory policy, but a distributive one.

There is also another assumption we need to underline: namely, that these contacts are place- and action-dependent. No nexus exists between specific local public spaces and the typology of contact, since most of the time it depends on the people who are in contact, their interests and intentions, as well as whether they know each other or not. But it is also obvious that some local public/private spaces, conventional/unconventional and informal/formal settings are more inviting to a certain type of contact than others. For instance, in public transport the contact is usually diversity-encounter, but if in the same public transport there is a racist explicit action, then the intercultural contact will take another form, either diversity-interaction (joint-action sharing a common concern) or diversity-solidarity (people will act with empathy, sharing the concern of the others). What is substantial for an intercultural citizenship approach is that each typology involves different social action theories.

Also important in this mapping exercise of conceptualizing intercultural citizenship's diversity-linkage theory is that we assume that we are aware of sharing a common space. This sharing space is substantial for the conception of intercultural citizenship, because most criticisms of multicultural citizenship have focused precisely on this territorialization of differences that prevent diversity-contacts in shared spaces. There cannot be intercultural citizenship if the space is segregated or dispersed. If intercultural citizenship contact can only naturally take place within shared spaces, then segregated schools, workplaces and housing can make this very difficult. Therefore policies need to be devised to try to make these spaces more inclusive. Shared spaces, then are then a substantial condition for intercultural citizenship. Especially within divided areas, it will be necessary to create opportunities to bring together members of different diversity-categories, for example the twinning of schools with children of different backgrounds, inter-faith discussions, or cultural events that embrace a range of cultures, perhaps using a variety of food or music to attract participants (see Cantle, 2008 for a range of cross-cultural activities). However, public spaces could also be created so that all communities can identify with them and are prepared to use them. These may be parks and gardens, town squares, public libraries and community halls, but they may often require redesigning to change the way in which they are seen and used (Nasser, 2015).

We now reach the last step of this rough conceptualization of intercultural citizenship's diversity-linkage theory. Compulsory questions need to be answered, such as what the optimal conditions are for contact promotion and what the factors are that prevent this contact. The negative drivers have already been set up: social inequalities, power relations within the diversity geography, prejudices and racism, xenophobic public narratives, and probably I would also add multicultural theoretical frameworks that tend to always differentiate and hence separate people into an us/other framework, instead of a having a 'together' narrative position. Among the positive drivers, I will underline equality conditions and power sharing as basic elements, but also at the structural level, positive media coverage on diversity-related news, positive public discourses and an educational curriculum that posits diversity as an advantage for our societies, and sharing spaces, as we have underlined above. We may also include the purpose of reducing what I have called elsewhere the 'diversity-gap', which points out the differences in terms of representation between the diversity of society and the diversity in several spheres of the society, basically spheres of power with a high degree of socialization function: schools, police, administrations and even political parties (Zapata-Barrero et al., 2018). It is now time to turn our eyes towards the normative drivers of intercultural citizenship.

6

NORMATIVE POLICY DRIVERS OF INTERCULTURAL CITIZENSHIP: A COMPREHENSIVE VIEW

INTRODUCTION: GUIDING QUESTIONS TO DISCUSS NORMATIVE DRIVERS OF INTERCULTURAL CITIZENSHIP

The core questions of this chapter are how intercultural citizenship justifies the need for policy intervention, and why this intervention needs to be focused on diversity-contact promotion. I will contend that there is not just one way to justify diversity intervention, but at least three: the social, political and cultural theories founding intercultural citizenship. Hence, I will use the '3D' expression, indicating not only that there are 3D(imensions), but 3D(rivers) that are interconnected. However, and as I will highlight, these can be implemented separately and indeed generate different kinds of intercultural citizenship debates. We now enter into the normative policy drivers sustaining intercultural citizenship.[1] Before properly beginning, let me underline that the three normative policy drivers need not be interpreted as being at odds, but rather as complementary angles of the same intercultural concern: the contractual, the cohesion and the constructivist strands. Each strand shares the idea that a policy intervention in the dynamics of diversity is necessary, although they have different ways of justifying this intervention. Hence, they generate different policy drivers, based on different particular empirical hypothesis and normative theories.

---

[1] Most of the arguments have been formulated in several works, the core one being the following article: Zapata-Barrero, R. (2016c).

After developing each policy driver, I will then defend the need to have a comprehensive view of intercultural citizenship, grounded on the argument that no one can have the sole authority to justify diversity-intervention through one intercultural lens, since the three strands can be applied at different moments, according to different purposes. The next challenge is for policy managers to be able to achieve a balance between the three normative policy drivers.

1. THREE HYPOTHESES ON DIVERSITY – WITHOUT INTERVENTION

The premise rests on the view that intercultural citizenship requires a policy intervention. Thus, the key question for us is how to justify diversity intervention (or, formulated in another way, how to justify intercultural promotion), rather than leaving the deployment of diversity to be carried out socially. The answer to this concern rests on three empirical hypotheses (3H), emerging from literature that focuses on the potential impacts of diversity without policy intervention.

The *political hypothesis* (H1) argues that diversity tends to alter the traditional expression of national identities, threatening traditional values and the rights and duties system of relations, which ensure a common sense of loyalty and stability between citizens and the basic structure of society. In this case, the technique of contact promotion seeks to maintain control of any justified change in traditional national values, protecting equilibrium between the loyalty of citizens and the rights of immigrants. This political concern is probably less local than national, since it is more an issue of national governance. At the local level it can also appear in concrete issues when cultural traditions are at stake in the debate, most of the time with a religious-based cultural heritage component, for instance the maintenance of a crucifix in a public square, or even the way a city hall develops a policy for Ramadan or Chinese New Year. This is basically the domain of the national tradition and involves the level of governance that has the competence to manage national tradition and values. This political concern is the main distinction of the intercultural view of Quebec (Bouchard, 2012) when we compare it with Europe, where intercultural citizenship is basically developed bottom-up, from the cities.

The *social hypothesis* (H2) says that diversity tends, at the beginning of the process, to provoke segregation and exclusion, and it reduces social capital and the sense of belonging in society, either through social inequalities or through the interference of information and knowledge among immigrants and citizens (Putnam, 2007). Through the use of social equality policies intercultural citizenship seeks to restore social cohesion, trust and feelings of belonging (Cantle, 2012). Intercultural citizenship complements these policies with policies that try to foster diversity-contacts (encounters, inter-dependencies, interactions and solidarity), knowledge formation and prejudice reduction.

The *cultural hypothesis* (H3) rests on the view that citizens' and immigrants' cultural capital are not fully developed in a diverse society. Here, I refer not only to nationality-based culture, but also to cultural citizenship in general (Zapata-Barrero, 2016d). Culture is one of the communication channels among people and a fundamental policy for intercultural citizenship. In a few words, culture keeps people together. This involves personal development, as a general process of intellectual, spiritual and aesthetic development, a way of life, and the works and practices of artistic activities (the three main dimensions of culture developed by the seminal work of Williams, 1976: 90). I am also using a Bourdieusian meaning of cultural capital (Bourdieu, 1979) as the set of cultural resources a person may have to develop his/her expectations, to network and with the capacity of transforming this resource into other forms of capital (economic, social). Bourdieu's concept of cultural capital refers to the collection of symbolic elements such as skills, tastes, posture, clothing, mannerisms, material belongings, credentials, etc. that one acquires through being part of a particular social class. Sharing similar forms of cultural capital with others – the same taste in movies, for example, or a football team – creates a sense of collective identity and group position ('people like us'). But Bourdieu also points out that cultural capital is a major source of social inequality. Certain forms of cultural capital are valued over others, and can help or hinder one's social mobility just as much as income or wealth.

Left alone, diversity tends to close off cultural opportunities. By intervening in diversity dynamics, intercultural citizenship seeks to promote the development, creativity and innovation of diverse societies (see, for instance, Bennett 2001). Immigrants have different cultural knowledge, religions, language, cultural skills, different conceptualizations and worldviews, personal artistic skills, and most of the time these cultural capabilities cannot be performed in current societies and may become a restraint, rather than a resource for increasing opportunities.

If we consider the 3H justifying diversity-intervention, we have indeed a 3D view of intercultural citizenship with three frameworks of potential diversity-contacts. First, there is a vertical diversity-related contact between persons and the basic structure of the society (the basis of the political hypothesis).

Second, there is a horizontal one among all the members of society, understood multidirectionally, but always diversity-related face-to-face relations (the basis of the social hypothesis). The third constitutes a deepening of interpersonal cultural development (the basis of the cultural hypothesis). Each hypothesis develops a theory that informs a distinct intercultural citizenship strand.

2. ZOOMING IN ON THE THREE NORMATIVE POLICY DRIVERS OF INTERCULTURAL CITIZENSHIP

To react to the *political hypothesis* (H1), we need to develop a *political theory of diversity* (D1). As the most recent illustration of this view I will take the work of Bouchard (2012), which is essentially centred on managing the relationship between diversity-related migrants and the basic structure of society, ensuring what Bouchard (2012: 229) calls 'the survival of national identity'.[2] D1 seeks to provide the most appropriate spaces for motivating agreements between national tradition, which accepts unavoidable changes, and the context of diversity, through participative policy channels and other means of vertical communication. This probably illustrates a most classical view of interculturalism, akin to international relations, as negotiation between unity and diversity, majority and minorities. This entails the need to manage the effect that the growing dynamics of diversity may have on the cultural tradition and national heritage that sustain a society and ensure stability. The policy informed by D1 will have, as its main target, to manage the potential impact that changes related to diversity-categories can have on tradition, to regulate the behaviour of nationals and to minimize the impacts on the loyalty of citizens and on the rights and duties of migrants (especially regarding equal opportunities).

Answering the *social hypothesis* requires the development of a *social theory of diversity* (D2) based on Cantle's (2008) view of interculturalism as community-cohesion. Supporting diversity-intervention through diversity-contact promotion involves transforming initial conflict zones into areas of positive contact, in order to ensure minimal welfare and quality of life. D2's basic aim is reducing/preventing the likelihood of social conflict, as diversity may become an explanatory factor of diversity-inequality and diversity power unbalance, and could instigate social conflicts (in a broader sense, encompassing racism, poverty and social exclusion; Cantle, 2012: 102). The promotion of social participation and

---

[2] As Bouchard highlights in previous work, this feeling is justified since it is an expression of the fragility of Francophone Quebec in America, a condition accentuated by globalization and by uncertainty over francization (Bouchard, 2011: 447).

the incorporation of immigrants into the mainstream social networks of the city are also main priorities in fostering cohesion. Territorial, social or whatever form exclusion may take, it is always considered as jeopardizing to one's condition of intercultural citizenship: to ensure shared spaces of diversity-contacts. Here there is an assumed premise that cohesion develops a sense of belonging and membership, so important for fostering intercultural citizenship

Finally, if we want to formulate policy reactions to the *cultural hypothesis*, we need to frame a *cultural theory of diversity* (D3), based on promoting the cultural capabilities of people, which is to be understood in terms of the cultural goods and resources needed to develop creative and innovative practices in society. This theory rests on a particular application of the diversity-advantage literature, which is already informing most of the diversity debate in Europe and elsewhere, introduced to the intercultural debate by Wood (2004) and Wood and Landry (2008). The policy following the intercultural citizenship narrative seeks to maximize the constructivist dimension of inter-personal contact, always seeking to produce something new as a product of diversity-contact.

Graphically speaking, the D1 seeks to legitimate a *contractual strand* of intercultural citizenship, having stability (of tradition and rights/duties) as its normative policy driver and the loss of national identity as its basic 'diversity limit'. The D2 shapes a *cohesion strand* of intercultural citizenship. It has 'cohesion' or 'social inclusion' as a normative policy driver and social conflict as its basic 'diversity limit'. Finally, the D3 is grounded in a *constructivist strand* of intercultural citizenship. It has development (of capabilities, innovation and creativity) as its normative policy driver, and the lack of equal capabilities (personal and social) as its basic 'diversity limit'.

In this picture, there are, then, 3D within the same intercultural triangle (see Figure 6.1).

To complete these analytical distinctions, let me now refer to the specific interface to which each D is dedicated.

D1: *Tradition/stability/diversity nexus:* The *contractual strand* understands intercultural citizenship as a function for enhancing stability in a diverse society, with tradition expressing itself through collective routines and socially 'acceptable' behaviours. It designates a set of established values and beliefs transmitted from generation to generation (Friedrich, 1972: 18), which can be interpreted as jeopardized by diversity dynamics. 'Tradition' is what Weber (1968: 29) conceptualized with the suggestive expression 'what has always existed'. In politics, tradition is also a framework for the unity of a community of citizens, and it is a tool for promoting a sense of loyalty, thus ensuring the preservation of social values. Tradition has an

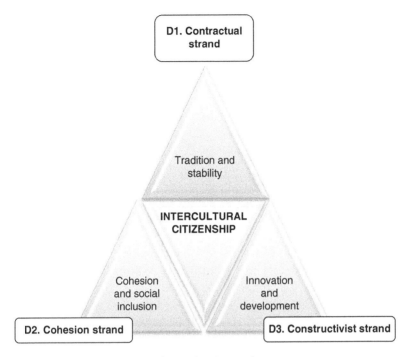

Figure 6.1 A comprehensive view of intercultural citizenship.

obvious social and political function, which plays an important role in the empowerment of national identity, ensuring its preservation. It is imperative to consolidate territorial routines and institutions, behaviour patterns and social action logics. Here the national values and civic practices sustaining traditions also play a prominent role. Tradition expresses itself through collective routines and socially acceptable behaviour. This does not mean that the contractual strand is against any change in traditional identity, but it contends rather that this cannot assume a loss of equilibrium between majority and minority nexus or an unbalance between Unity and Diversity, which are still present as interpretative theoretical frameworks.

When this tradition becomes ideology, it can ground the conservative nationalist political discourse (which is obviously not necessarily linked to the conservative right wing), in the literal sense of seeking to preserve tradition against processes of change due to new dynamics of diversity. This does not mean that one is against any change of traditional identity, but rather that one contends that this change cannot assume a loss of power and authority in managing the dynamics of tradition in the majority/minority nexus. There are, then, two constant concerns in the contractual intercultural citizenship view: the preservation of the national identity and respect for the rights of the still so-called 'minorities' when speaking of migrant-related individuals. Hence, this contractual strand is closely related to liberal nationalism, as clearly defended by, among others, Miller (2008). For instance, the basic pillar of Bouchard's contractual view as *equilibrium* rests on this point. He insists, once again, that this framework must not be interpreted in conflictive terms, but rather as a dynamic equilibrium of contact. The presence of 'minorities' means that all forms of expressions of difference become defined in relation to the national culture or founder majority. For instance, Bouchard says categorically that the majority/minority nexus in Quebec seems unavoidable and non-negotiable as a framework for analysis (Bouchard, 2012: 162, 167). In this case this strand is still driven by ethnic and racial views of diversity, and in this sense, it has many affinities with multicultural citizenship and even civic-national citizenship. It is in fact the way most multiculturalists interpret interculturalism (see, for instance, Modood, 2016). For the *contractual strand*, 'contact' is basically conceived in *vertical terms*, between a founding majority culture and a diverse culture of 'minorities'. In this view, contact is seen as a strategy of negotiations between identities, and it presumes a homogeneous view of both parts of the interaction (national citizens vs. diverse immigrants).

Ultimately, the contractual view seems to promote some sort of *reconciliation* between a national majority and a diverse minority.[3] As a guiding thread in this line of thought, Bouchard insists that 'interculturalism commits majority / minority in an opening and reconciliation dynamic rather than retrenchment and tensions' (2012: 64).[4] The question here is, how to attenuate the dualism respecting the rights of people: interculturalism is always understood as a way to arbitrate conflicts and divisions, as a way to promote living together in a divided society (2012: 89).

---

[3]Even if this term has a quite concrete meaning for Québécois, illustrating a way to restore past conflicts between Quebec national founders and indigenous autochthones, the term 'reconciliation' has been used in some reports within this context of immigration-related diversity. See, for instance, the same Bouchard-Taylor report (2008), whose subtitle states: *Fonder l'avenir. Le temps de la reconciliation* (*Building the Future – A Time for Reconciliation*).

[4]Translation from French by the author.

D2: *Cohesion/social inclusion/diversity nexus:* The *cohesion strand* understands intercultural citizenship as a tool for managing the social inclusion/dynamics of the diversity nexus. It sees intercultural citizenship as a way to promote community cohesion (Cantle, 2001). In contrast with the contractual strand, this view builds arguments without any national concern, since it is understood that the nation upholds state mechanisms already in place to deal with national protection. This is not to say that there is no debate on, let's say, Britishness, Frenchness, Italianness, but it is not considered from the cohesion view. Rather, the basic worries are social conflict and segregation, due chiefly to the lack of communication among different expressions of diversity (including the national citizenship one). The intercultural strategy is interpreted as a policy mechanism for generating trust and mutual understanding, and for breaking down prejudices, stereotypes and the misconceptions of others. We might say it is a technique of bridging and bonding differences and social capital. That is, it promotes relations between people who share certain characteristics (bonds), as well as relations between individuals from different backgrounds (such as promoting contact between people across different religions, languages, etc.) (Gruescu and Menne, 2010: 10). It is a way, then, to avoid the confinement and segregation of people, which, as a last resort, become explanatory variables of social exclusion and social inequality, especially in neighbourhoods and cities. Social cohesion is also the horizon in the sense that it encourages inter-personal contact to overcome social and cultural barriers among people, especially in neighbourhoods and cities (Cantle, 2012: 103), with the final aim to restore a cohesive community. Cantle also draws a link between programmes promoting inter-personal contact and programmes of belonging that cannot be dismissed, in the sense that to ensure the permanence of cohesion, there is a need to promote a minimal sense of belonging.

The cohesion strand addresses power relations as well, particularly in terms of tackling inequalities, both in opportunities and in outcomes. The purpose here is to work on the pre-conditions of mutual respect prior to intercultural contact, so that when 'contact' is made it is more likely to be effective (Allport, 1954). Therefore, in contrast to the contractual strand, it promotes better face-to-face relations, step by step, in a context of proximity. Cantle, for instance, explicitly speaks about local identity and belonging campaigns to garner a sense of solidarity. We might say that while feelings of common values were the connection in past periods, it is now necessary to focus on a shared space of contact. From the perspective of cohesion, it tends to bridge the tension between being 'too diverse' (Goodhart, 2004) and being cohesive.

For the *cohesion strand* this contact is basically understood in horizontal terms. It is always multidimensional and complex, without any pre-categorization of the population. It thus breaks away the dualistic view of the population, as the contractual strand still maintains a *majority-us-national-citizen* and a *minority-other-diverse-immigrant*. In this case, and again in contrast with the contractual strand, it is in line with the post-ethnic and post-racial view of diversity, and probably closer to the current post-M period in which we have placed intercultural citizenship.

D3: *The innovation/development/diversity nexus:* The *constructivist strand* understands intercultural citizenship as a method for managing the innovation/development and diversity nexus. It sees intercultural policy as an instrument for promoting innovation and development in a diverse society. It has then basically a proactive dimension, in the sense that it is not a policy thought to react against any negative outcome of diversity (as a therapeutic policy), but is instead concentrated on producing a new outcome as a product of interaction. It is, then, creativity-based. This driver of construction is, therefore, its distinguishing characteristic. This view of diversity is perhaps best expressed by Page (2007), who states that in a problem-solving situation, heterogeneous groups have better tools to provide a variety of responses than homogeneous ones. He then provides an empirical argument for why contact in diversity can be an asset to society. This view of diversity as an asset highlights the fact that through inter-personal contact, something new is potentially generated. Both the former contractual and cohesion strands miss this added value of diversity. Expressing itself in the form of innovation and creativity, this constructivist approach also has a different view of diversity. Diversity is basically considered as an opportunity for promoting individual and social development/innovation. From this point of view, policies informed by the intercultural citizenship narrative can then be considered as a strategy that promotes a context of mutual development.[5] This constructivist view takes a step forward, in the sense that it promotes the cultural capabilities of people. I am here more sympathetic to the conception of equality put forward by the Nobel Prizewinner Amartya Sen (2010),

---

[5]This is maybe the view best worked by the Intercultural Cities programme of the Council of Europe (2011a), which shows through many case studies that cities can take diversity as an asset for individual and social development. See, among others, reports on diverse cities: London (Bagwell et al., 2012), Lewisham (a borough of London) (Brecknock et al., 2007) and Helsinki (Comedia, 2010). Regarding Barcelona, a more recent critical article has appeared in Zapata-Barrero (2014).

when he argues that governments should be measured against the concrete capabilities of their citizens. This capability approach of diversity obviously has a direct impact on some categories of the other two interpretative strands.

First of all, it sees people not only as national-agents (as in the contractual strand), or simply as human beings (as in the cohesion strand), but as capable agents. This involves people not only being considered in terms of their rights, but also in terms of what they can do and are able to achieve. We take into consideration, then, individual skills (what an individual knows how to do) and competences (what an individual is capable of doing). In fact, this view has the potential of giving answers to a question which the contractual and cohesion strands have not even posed, and which seems to me commonsensical. It is not a question focused on the function of intercultural citizenship, such as why positive inter-personal diversity-contact matters, but rather concerns the incentives of people to engage in contact with other people. Namely, how are people motivated to contact other people from different diversity backgrounds? It is fair to recognize that in spite of sharing the core equation 'intercultural citizenship = positive contact = diversity-contact', each strand has different notions of what contact assumes and means in social and functional terms.

Definitively, depending on the perspective we underline, the contractual strand can be considered as a national-based view of intercultural citizenship, while the cohesion strand is much more cosmopolitan as it leaves aside the national view of the population as the only criterion to define its diversity. In this way it has an expansive view of diversity, as super-diversity. Finally, the constructivist strand has a transformative-based view of intercultural citizenship. Likewise, we can also point out that for both the cohesion and the contractual strands, intercultural citizenship is understood as a tool for preventing national divisions (D1) and social conflicts (D2). D1 sees the new diversity dynamics as potential threats to tradition (the *contractual strand*); D2 perceives diversity dynamics as new potential factors of poverty and exclusion (D2). The *constructivist strand*, in its turn, sees this new population as an opportunity for innovation. We take this category in the most literal sense as involving creativity, transformation, change, alteration, modification, renovation, modernization, and even performance and improvement. As different from tradition – to modify the previous Weberian expression – it promotes 'what never existed' but can be generated through diversity-contact processes. This is what the different categories of diversity may produce through contact promotion: something new for all agents. Moreover, like any new component in society, it transforms the context for everyone involved; it accommodates diversity, creates new spaces for action, and alters the existing logic of action. Therefore, regarding innovation, what primarily matters is the transformative effect it produces, which is absent in both the *contractual* and *cohesion* strands.

Incorporating this 3D of intercultural citizenship, we can say graphically that stability (of tradition, rights), cohesion (regarding social conflict) and development (of capabilities, innovation and creativity) become an interpretative framework within which we can draw the different narratives of intercultural citizenship. What is most important is that these views are only complementary angles. Indeed, it is this comprehensive view that I will defend as the final step in my argumentation.

3. INTERCULTURAL CITIZENSHIP: A COMPREHENSIVE APPROACH

The comprehensive approach is the main basis for the normative foundations of intercultural citizenship. This global view holds that intercultural citizenship is a way to manage the contractual (tradition-based), cohesion (social inclusion-based) and constructivist (innovation-based) policy strands. To understand this comprehensive view appropriately, we have to keep in mind that intercultural citizenship should be performance oriented. I propose widening the focus to see all three views at the same time, as interconnected. Indeed, my substantial argument is that when intercultural citizenship is implemented, it should have as a horizon neither the contractual, nor the cohesion, nor the constructivist views alone, but the 3D applied at different moments in the city, according to particular purposes and needs.

This interplay between tradition, cohesion and innovation is thus the framework within which we can ground the intercultural citizenship narrative. This involves policies, behaviours, cultural practices, institutional routines and management programmes that help create bridges between 'what has always existed' (contractual strand), 'what generates social conflicts' (cohesion strand) and 'what has never existed' (constructivist strand). It ultimately works to apply this logic of equilibrium that has been so insistently defended by Bouchard's *contractual philosophy*, and this anti-exclusion logic orienting Cantle's *cohesion view*, but with the added value of innovation, creativity and human and social development. Without this added value, intercultural citizenship can become, in this scenario, just a phase in the historical trajectory of diversity in society, and would not reach the level of becoming a new policy paradigm. The real challenge of intercultural citizenship is not to decide which of these 3D is right or wrong, but to balance them in a comprehensive framework, one that considers that the techniques of contact-promotion must create a context where tradition, cohesion and innovation drive local governments' intercultural policies and politics.

7

REPUBLICANISM, PUBLIC SPACE AND INTERCULTURAL CITIZENSHIP

INTRODUCTION: THE CONTEXT OF INTERCULTURAL CITIZENSHIP'S PRACTICE – PUBLIC SPACES

Diversity dynamics brings new and old ways of using public spaces, strengthening its important socializing role, and thereby bringing about new complexities that need to be tackled. It is in public spaces that we can stimulate diversity-contacts transforming this public domain either in conflict zones or simply contact zones. The practical idea I want to raise in this chapter is how to use the potential of public space for intercultural citizenship promotion. I would just like to remind the reader that intercultural citizenship has two main strengths: the first is diversity-awareness and recognition by all citizens living in society, and the second is the predisposition to share public space. In absence of a shared space, diversity-contacts simply cannot happen. Public space offers this shared ground and facilitates the socialization processes (Kihato et al., 2010) of cultural exchange and learning required by intercultural citizenship. Public space is where all citizens, regardless of their income, personal circumstances and diversity-categories, can feel equal. Public spaces are where people can meet, socialize, discover common likes and passions, affirm their shared rights to the city, organize, and where they can participate in neighbourhood activities and defend commonly held rights or demands (Garau, 2014: 10). Unfortunately, the quality of public spaces varies among and even within most cities.

There has been much debate about definitions of public space: where we draw the lines between public and private, inside or outside, restrictive or free, secure or insecure, equitable or otherwise. We can start with the descriptive definition provided by the United Nations Educational, Scientific and Cultural Organization (UNESCO) (2018): 'A public space refers to an area or place that is open and accessible to all peoples, regardless of gender, race, ethnicity, age or socioeconomic level.' Spatial urban planning should take the opportunity to enhance intercultural citizenship practices. Carr et al. (1993) distinguishes 11 types of public spaces: public parks, squares and plazas, memorials, markets, streets, playgrounds, community open spaces, greenways and parkways, atrium/indoor market places, found spaces/everyday spaces and waterfronts. But it can also be neighbourhood spaces like the residential streets, or forecourts (Dines et al., 2006). We can also add community gardens, libraries, public amenities, festivals and neighbourhood spaces, as reported by Bagwell et al. (2012). Connecting spaces, such as sidewalks and streets, are also public spaces. In the twenty-first century, some even consider the virtual spaces available through the internet as a new type of public space that develops interaction and social mixing. For UNESCO, public spaces can play a key role in improving migrants' inclusion by acting as places for intercultural exchange. Segregated areas can be opened up thanks to careful physical planning interventions. It is in fact this non-excludable nature of public space that makes the development of intercultural citizenship possible. It is also possible to discriminate on access to streets, sidewalks, public gardens, playgrounds and parks. Public spaces constitute a resource that should be accessible to all, including old and new migrants (Peters et al., 2010).

To my knowledge the multicultural literature has not yet deployed any lines of research on how to deal with diversity in public spaces, the 'shared zone' *par excellence*. The multicultural citizenship narrative has been rather inclined to problematize the public sphere, interpreted as being the institutionalization of sameness (e.g. Parekh, 2000; Young, 1990). The concern over how to manage diversity-contacts in public spaces has also been neglected by the civic-nationalist narrative agenda.

The importance of mobilizing public spaces at the level of neighbourhoods can become imperative under circumstances in which areas that are left alone may be at risk of being managed by the market, following its consumption's logic of action, rather than that of social aims and public goods (Wood, 2015), and even become the concrete space of insecurity and diversity-related discriminations. One additional problem today is that public spaces are sometimes represented as spaces of insecurity, isolation, threat, danger, conflicts, of consumption and competition, and other features that prevent diversity-contacts (Calhoun, 1992). There is also a criticism of the privatization of public spaces that may be relevant for us. The disappearance of open public spaces can generate negative social consequences and launch a spiral of decline. As the vibrancy of public spaces diminishes we lose the habit of participating in street life. The natural policing of streets that comes from the presence of people needs to be replaced by 'security' and the city itself becomes less free and more alienating. These public domain retreats are also a structural cause of lack of contact zones for diversity-contact promotion that we have to take into account (Rogers, 2008). One condition for making public spaces work for intercultural citizenship, then, is to make sure they are safe spaces where people can celebrate their cultural peers with autonomy (Knapp, 2007). Most of the conditions for enhancing intercultural citizenship from the diversity-linkage theory I have sketched previously (in Chapter 5) take place in such public spaces.

If there is a tradition of thought with which intercultural citizenship can be identified, it is the classical tradition of republicanism originating in Aristotle. Accordingly, politics finds its authentic expression whenever citizens gather together in a public space to deliberate and decide about matters of collective concern. Political activity is valued not because it may lead to agreement or to a shared conception of the good, but because it enables each citizen to exercise his or her powers of agency, to develop the capacities for judgement (Passerin d'Entreves, 2018), and to attain a sense of place and belonging. For the republican tradition, public space is the space of politics, of public opinion, of participation, communication and practice, where citizenship is formed and practised (Honohan, 2017). Citizenship mainly denotes practices of engagement, relational activities and deliberations in the public sphere, through which citizens organize and articulate their claims. For the republican tradition, we have a moral responsibility to create physical places that facilitate public engagement and diversity-contacts. It is first a direct criticism of the process of disappearance of public life, well described by Gehl and Rogers (2010: 27–8) when saying:

> In a society becoming steadily more privatized with private homes, cars, computers, offices and shopping centres, the public component of our lives is disappearing. It is more and more important to make the cities inviting, so we can meet our fellow citizens face to face and experience directly through our senses. Public life in good quality public spaces is an important part of a democratic life and a full life.

Intercultural citizenship can here be seen as a 'local protection' against other invading logics into the public space, or even against racist behaviour or xenophobic attitudes (Zapata-Barrero, 2015a).

Before going on to conceptualize public space and intercultural citizenship, let me place this discussion within citizenship studies. The purpose is to defend the fact that intercultural citizenship, in spite of having features of liberal and communitarian traditions, digs out its distinction from the republican tradition in its defence of public space and the fundamental idea that citizenship can only be reached through practice.

In section 1 I will roughly present the three traditions of citizenship, with the purpose of framing intercultural citizenship within the republican tradition. Then in section 2 I will change my prism and adopt the republican lens to further explore the urban spatiality and place-making of intercultural citizenship. Then, with the literature from urban studies, I will go into section 3 to discuss the people-to-place linkages. Finally, in section 4 I will close this republican defence of intercultural citizenship, discussing the conditions for the use of public spaces.

1. THE PLACE OF PUBLIC SPACES WITHIN THE THREE TRADITIONS OF CITIZENSHIP: THE REPUBLICAN VIEW OF INTERCULTURAL CITIZENSHIP[1]

Citizenship studies tend to designate at least three main conceptions of citizenship:[2] a liberal, a communitarian and a republican conception. In the *liberal tradition*, the state frames citizenship. This basically means that we need a state to organize citizenship. A national without a state, despite claiming a certain national identity, could not claim citizenship. From this liberal view, the state has complete sovereignty regarding how to conceptually delimit citizenship, for instance through a naturalization process if non-citizens request citizenship. It is well known that the liberal tradition has a rights-based approach towards citizenship. Following Marshall's distinctions, we can define citizenship as a set of civic, political and social rights, with voting being one the most distinctive. It is, of course, the state that has the responsibility to distribute these rights. The liberal tradition promotes

---

[1] I summarize the main review from Zapata-Barrero (2016d).

[2] As obviously there is a big array of literature, I will concentrate mainly on those that I think outline the most important arguments and perspectives: Isin and Turner (2002); Stevenson (2003).

citizenship basically as equal status and position in society. Those who hold this status are allowed to do certain things that non-citizens cannot do.

Communitarianism has a different view. It is not the state, but the nationality that frames citizenship. From this point of view, even if a state is not behind it, nationality functions to keep people together, as it is strengthened as a common project towards the future. It means the sharing of a minimum of historical narrative and national construction, or a common inter-generational link, determined by descent and ethnicity. Whatever the criterion is, what shapes citizenship is a shared national identity. Through citizenship, the national community feeling is reinforced. We are here very close to the concept of 'community of citizens', established some years ago by Schnapper (1998). Communitarian citizenship means that people feel that they can participate in this national identity-building process through their community interrelations. The communitarian tradition has a national membership-based approach to citizenship. This basically means that its primary concern is to ensure that the loyalty of citizens is channelled through a minimal common sharing of national membership. Belonging to the community can help people to orient their expectations and to direct their life. Citizenship without this feeling of national membership is difficult to sustain.

For the *republican tradition*, it is neither the state nor the nationality that frames citizenship, but the public space. What is shared here is not a set of equal rights (liberal tradition), or a feeling of national membership (the root of communitarian citizenship), but the space of action: the public sphere. It is the practice in public space that gives meaning to citizenship. If the public space is restricted, it becomes a space of competition or crime, then it is the same republican tradition that suffers. We see that, in contrast with the other two traditions, citizenship is determined not by who has the 'monopoly' over the definition (the state), nor by a distinctive sense of community (the national identity), but rather by a sphere of everyday experience and action. This is why we can say that, for the republican tradition, 'citizen' is the answer to the question of 'Who am I?' when it is posed in the public sphere. The republican tradition seeks to involve citizens in public affairs and in the making of society. This public engagement comes from the requirement that people take responsibility and that they limit individual interests in favour of public ones.

It follows that each citizenship tradition invites different kinds of behaviours that are relevant for placing intercultural citizenship's distinctive features within the republican tradition. The difference between active and passive citizens is very common in citizenship studies. Here, we find that both the liberal and communitarian traditions share a passive view of citizenship. This means that people do not need to engage in order to be citizens, since they hold this status or membership by adscription. This lack of visible behaviour is unthinkable for the republican tradition, which only defines citizenship by its active role, public engagement and shared practices. It follows that both the liberal and communitarian traditions agree in their views that citizenship is initially acquired by birth or later achieved through naturalization. In contrast, the republican tradition insists that 'a person is not born a citizen, but becomes a citizen' (Rousseau). Here, the socialization process plays a functional role for citizenship behaviour, one of the core elements of intercultural citizenship.

I am aware that it is risky to try to encapsulate intercultural citizenship within a citizenship tradition, but I will contend that even if it is necessary to hold many liberal and communitarian views of citizenship, one of its distinctive features is certainly republicanism. The republican premise is then that one is not an intercultural citizen, but becomes one. Intercultural citizenship views public space as a diversity-contact zone, and it is based on everyday personal experiences in diversity settings. A republican intercultural citizenship concern is to ensure an appropriate framework for diversity-contacts and prevent the expansion of barriers for diversity-encounters, diversity-interdependencies, diversity-interactions and diversity-solidarity practices (the four main diversity-contact dimensions put forward in Chapter 5).

Taken from the republican tradition we can say that intercultural citizenship is a narrative that can perfectly shape a politics of the public space. Diversity policies have often assumed this environment-awareness, so important for the republican conceptualization of public spaces in diversity settings. This necessarily involves a reflection on the making of society, socio-spatial practices and a new public culture, a culture of diversity.

2. REPUBLICANISM PROVIDES TO INTERCULTURAL CITIZENSHIP A REFLECTION OF URBAN SPATIALITY AND PLACE-MAKING

Intercultural citizenship requires daily coexistence with difference in what Amin (2002) has called the banal 'micro-publics' of the city, the everyday spaces where people share some common projects, whether that be in a community centre, a community garden or a neighbourhood house. It involves shared activities, not simply the disengaged sharing of public space. Intercultural citizenship can then become a new form of social and spatial belonging (Sandercock, 2003).

The republican tradition of citizenship helps us, then, to stress the role space and spatiality play in intercultural citizenship formation. In fact intercultural citizenship can be viewed as a 'spatial experience'. The centrality that this spatial experience plays in human relations has been rightly labelled as 'spatial turn' (Warf and Arias, 2008). The central argument here is that that space itself is not a given, but it is a socially produced entity which is created, understood and experienced differently by different people at different times. This spatial experience involves cognitive and behavioural dimensions (Russell, 2015: 1–24). Movements through the space are limited by the interaction of the body and the physical form of the space.

It is through this 'spatiality experience' that republican citizenship develops most of its distinguishing features: actions, experiences, social exchanges, learning processes, cultural exchange and intercultural practices. The normalization of the dynamics of diversity has brought about, amongst other factors, new and old ways of being and using the 'spatial experience' and its socializing role, thereby bringing about new complexities that need to be tackled by the intercultural citizenship narrative.

Some empirical studies have already shown whether public spaces facilitate inclusion and intercultural communication that may transcend ethnocultural divisions and traditional public/private boundaries (Galanakis, 2013). Intercultural citizenship, in this sense, refers to the possibility of allowing different people from different backgrounds to use the same space. It has been nicely described by Gehl (2011) as 'life between buildings'. From the republican tradition, what makes a space public is not its preordained 'publicness', but rather that some people make it public through actions and practices. I take here Amin's argument (2009: 11) that practices in public spaces are formed pre-cognitively rather than rationally and consciously, guided by routines rather than by acts of human will. We can here apply Bourdieu's term of 'habitus'. It refers to the physical embodiment of cultural capital, to the deeply ingrained habits, skills and dispositions that we possess due to our life experiences.

Behind this, there is a focus on place-making, which capitalizes on a local community's potential with the intention of creating public spaces that promote people's health, happiness and well-being. Place-making is both a process and a philosophy (Schneekloth and Shibley, 1995). This follows the premise that intercultural public spaces can fundamentally contribute to the quality of life of individuals and society.

When speaking about republicanism as the main dimension of intercultural citizenship we focus particularly on what Lofland (1998: 63ff) describes as *person-to-place connections*. Lofland looks at three 'ways' in which places matter to people, three forms of connection and to develop place attachments:

(a) 'Memorialized Locales' refers to small pieces of the public realm that – because of events that happened and/or because of some object (e.g. a statue) that resides within them – take on, for some people, the aura of 'sacred places'; (b) 'Familiarized Locales: Paths/Rounds/Ranges' refers to locales that people encounter or move through on a daily or almost daily basis and with which they establish a familiar relationship; (c) 'Hangouts and Home Territories' – the one person-to-place connection that has been the recipient of much social science attention is that between people and their 'home territories'.

Diverse cities, therefore, are always stimulating because they are rich in 'intercultural spatial experiences', in contrast to homogeneous cities, which can scarcely avoid being poor in intercultural experiences. The republican dimension of intercultural citizenship therefore mirrors what Mitchell (2003) describes as the right to the city, that is, the right to presence, to occupy public space and participate as an equal. Intercultural citizenship can then be interpreted as a defence of freely accessible public spaces for everyone, as a condition for all forms of contacts.

3. PUBLIC SPACES' SOCIAL ASSETS: PEOPLE-TO-PLACE LINKAGES IN DIVERSITY SETTINGS

Even if it sounds a bit rhetorical, for the republican intercultural citizenship 'public spaces are space of the public' (Mitchell, 2003). This intrinsic relationship between people and places can be best explained by Walzer's (1986: 470) remarks made some time ago in his reflection on complex justice. There he said that a public space is a

> space we share with strangers, people who aren't our relatives, friends, or work associates. It is a space for politics, religion, commerce, sports; space for peaceful coexistence and impersonal encounters. Its character expresses and conditions our public life, civic cultures, and everyday discourse.

These premises allow him to shape urban space into two distinct groups that may be analytically relevant for our discussions: 'single-minded' and 'open-minded' spaces. 'Single-minded' describes a concept of urban space that fulfils a single function. 'Open-minded' is conceived as multi-functional fashioning of a variety of uses in which everyone can participate. The residential suburb, the housing estate, the business district, the industrial zone, the car park, ring-road, shopping mall, even the car itself, provide 'single-minded' spaces. But the busy square, the lively street, the market, the park, the pavement café are 'open-minded'. When we are in the first type of spaces we are generally in a hurry, but in the 'open-minded' places we are ready to meet people.

Both categories can play a role in intercultural citizenship, but it definitely has most affinities with 'open-minded' spaces. Single-minded spaces satisfy our modern desire for private consumption and individualism. In contrast, open-minded places bring diversity dynamics of society together and engender a culture of diversity, with a corresponding sense of tolerance, place awareness, identity and mutual respect. It is open-minded public spaces and the experiences people have there that can inspire feelings of belonging and safety (Galanakis, 2013). Urbanists have long held the view that the physical and social dynamics of public space play a central role in the formation of public culture (Amin, 2009: 5). Hence this relation between intercultural citizenship, republican tradition, public space and spatial practice is meaningful for producing a culture of diversity, which we have defined as incorporating diversity-awareness, diversity-recognition and diversity-participation. I also include safety since some empirical studies show that people have the will to use and interact in public spaces if they have the feeling of safety (Wood and Landry, 2008).

Inclusion and exclusion of public spaces play an analytical function here which I also need to underline. Intercultural citizenship is basically inclusion in non-private spaces. The protection of public spaces from private interests can then become an intercultural citizenship policy, since it seeks to protect one of the conditions of contact: to ensure an open-minded and non-hierarchical space. This is directly connected with the most popular definition of the public domain in contrast with the private realm, which points out the access opportunities (Lofland, 1998: 8; Madanipour, 1996: 146). There is here a longstanding set of debates regarding the importance of public space for the flourishing of democratic, representative, heterogeneous cities (Hall, 2012; Iveson, 2007; Mitchell, 2003; Sennett, 2012). Habermas' (1991) concept of the public sphere links its emergence with the development of democracy, and this is the premise of most research on public spaces (Carr et al., 1993; Gehl and Matan, 2009).

The meaning of public space is then rooted in its assets, its provision and use. Studies have shown that the physical setting of a public space can influence its meaning for social interaction and for fostering a sense of community (see Madanipour, 2010; Peters, 2011). By appropriating spaces that are overlooked by other urban residents as socializing spaces, migrants are circumventing official policy, marking their presence in the city (Collins, 2012). For us, the fact that public spaces are the proper spaces of intercultural citizenship practice means foremost that they are spaces where we can encourage diversity-contacts and celebrate diversity, and they are here that the learning process of diversity-recognition takes place. Undoubtedly, there remains great precariousness in the lives of low-waged migrants where strong and sometimes abusive relations of power occur in everyday life and reflect diversity-interpersonal attitudes and practices. Thus, while these instances of appropriation do not directly or permanently challenge broader inequalities, such practices of claiming space are important precisely because they allude to the different specialized forms of coexisting with difference in the city (Ye, 2017: 5).

Public spaces can be sites of huge intercultural opportunity. Organized events, such as football matches, festivals or youth group activities, may offer important opportunities for diversity-contacts and for generating shared spatial experiences. Migrants tend to use open public spaces, community gardens and parks to gather and congregate in ways that are reminiscent of their home country, transforming the parks of their adoptive community into familiar spaces, creating an 'autotopography' that links their daily practices and life experiences to a deep sense of place (Agyeman, 2017).

Public spaces are sometimes age- and generation-dependent. Young people are usually their greatest occupiers. Through leisure activities, for instance, public spaces become the main spaces of communication for youth and at the same time spaces of socialization that may compete with traditional spaces such as schools and family. Public spaces are spaces of friendship, of culture's consumption and production. In fact, for young people, when culture and public spaces meet it produces a main space for diverse contacts and inclusion as well as a space to foster cultural citizenship for young people (Zapata-Barrero, 2016d). When practices of public space provoke repetition and frequency, they then become a place youth develop trust for, affection and recognition (Neal et al., 2015: 469), and even feelings of belonging, which occurs through the appropriation of public spaces. When public spaces are circumscribed, such as green parks or market places, they become spaces of chatting and encounters, and even a degree of social intimacy. A successful public space is then a space that gives opportunities to participate in communal cultural activities. The influential work of Carr et al. (1993) put it straightforwardly:

> In the parks, plazas, markets, waterfronts, and natural areas of our cities, people from different cultural groups can come together in a supportive context of mutual enjoyment. As these experiences are repeated, public spaces become vessels to carry positive communal meanings. (1993: 344)

Intercultural citizenship develops some other social assets in public spaces. It includes 'togetherness', social affinities afforded by sharing temporary, repeatedly on-going spaces generating engagement that can be interpreted as social routines. In contrast with the street encounter, the park, for instance, elevates the contact from an awareness/acknowledgement of difference to an experience of connection and shared affinity for the park itself. It is a place that is purposively sought for enjoyment and pleasure (Neal et al., 2015: 473)

We have to take into account that public spaces can be used in a diversity of ways, by different people, and can even be experienced differently by people from different categories of diversity. For example, Neal et al. (2015: 465) showed at least 13 categories of park activities and practices: fresh air, relaxing, taking children out, exercise, meeting friends, being where other people are, seeing nature, eating and picnicking, etc. Organized park events and celebratory occasions – fun days, festivals, and fetes, were particularly identified as moments of diversity-contacts. Another example of research of public parks argues that African-Americans and Hispanics have a different understanding and use of public parks (Low et al., 2006). Most Hispanics come to the park accompanied by family members and are typically encountered in groups. When at the park, they are likely to get involved in gregarious uses including parties, celebrations of birthdays, wedding anniversaries and picnics (Loukaitou-Sideris, 1995: 94; see also Low et al., 2006: Part 1).

4. CONDITIONS FOR THE USE OF INTERCULTURAL PUBLIC SPACES

This last example allows us to underline one basic condition for the use of public spaces by republican intercultural citizenship: there is autonomy for people to meet their cultural peers (creating a diverse public space) or have social contact with other people holding diverse categories, as diversity-contact, and even 'inbetweenness', as Ye puts it (2017). Taking the eight lessons for promoting diversity in public spaces from Knapp (2007), another condition is that people need to recognize the culture within public space and feel their culture is represented through familiar symbols. Put another way, when people do not see their values and preferences reflected in a place, they feel unwelcome. Diversity-representation plays a prominent role here, since it can favour or not favour diversity-participation in public spaces. This also means that public spaces need to be a discrimination-free zone, free from hostilities and diversity-related conflicts. Studies show how discrimination may discourage the use of public parks, civic centres and other places. Self-restraint and self-prevention from going to certain public spaces by black-skinned people because they feel unwelcome must also be a target for intercultural citizenship. This is why diverse public spaces need to be welcoming public spaces. The physical proximity of diverse populations in spaces such as buses, parks, public squares has the potential to generate hostility as much as conviviality (Ye, 2017). Such affirmative assessments of physical proximities of people from diverse cultural, social or ethnic backgrounds that seem to embody city life have long been, of course, accompanied by equally strong critical accounts of contact. This line of argument also highlights that transient encounters, even of a positive nature, do not necessarily 'scale up', that is, develop any lasting challenge to embedded prejudices and stereotypes. Valentine and colleagues' more recent work has continued to show how mundane and routine forms of sharing space are embedded with acts and justifications of prejudice against people of different backgrounds (Valentine et al., 2015). By affording safety to public spaces, the republican dimension ensures that people will choose to use them.

Placing emphasis on the inter-dependency between public spaces and social dynamics of inter-personal contact, the public space has to be understood not only as communicating space (Habermas, 1991), but has to include corporeal body and streets' micro-movements (Watson, 2006), such as glances at the bus stops. It is also the space where most of the 'sensitive proximity' (Simmel, 2009) and emotions related to diversity take place, where negative and positive feelings of connections occur. In addition there are spaces where social exclusion and social ordering take place, and they are also environments that the government seeks to securitize and police.

The geography of togetherness through the sharing of space already has a long story, beginning with analyses of co-presence and contact (Ye, 2017). The republican reading of these reflections allows us to underline once more the importance of the scale of the city and neighbourhood in implementing intercultural citizenship. It is this public space that contextualizes the statement of living together in diversity. How do societies establish civility, then conviviality, across difference? Let me add some features of intercultural citizenship, when it is explored from the public space perspective. Lofland (1998: 10) speaks about the 'parochial realm' characterized by a sense of commonality among acquaintances and neighbours who are involved in inter-personal networks that are located within 'communities'. The parochial realm is the world of the neighbourhood, workplace or acquaintance networks; and the public realm is the world of strangers and the 'street' (persons who are personally unknown to one another). The word strangers has been reserved almost exclusively to mean 'cultural strangers' (those who occupy symbolic worlds different from our own, who do not necessarily share our values, history or world perspective) rather than 'biographical strangers' (one who moves into a world of many who are unknown or only categorically known to them) (Lofland, 1998: 9).

The republican tradition features new dimensions to the intercultural citizenship approach. In fact, and following again Amin's (2009) seminal focus, there is a strong connection between public space and *demos*. From this perspective public spaces shape the intercultural citizenship potential for public participation, mass political, religious and cultural gatherings, solidarity practices and building public identity. Intercultural citizenship will then involve measures to bring diverse people together in shared spaces or common ventures. Conviviality becomes also a keyword. Amin (2009: 18–19) says that 'conviviality is identified as an important everyday virtue of living with difference'. In our terms, conviviality involves that we share 'spatial experience' in public space.

8

THE SOCIAL BENEFITS OF INTERCULTURAL CITIZENSHIP: DIVERSITY AS A PUBLIC GOOD

INTRODUCTION: DIVERSITY AS A PUBLIC GOOD

The production of social benefits is consubstantial with intercultural citizenship. This is directly related to its distinctive view of diversity as a public good, as an asset and a resource that may be beneficial for the society. This approach, usually anchored under the umbrella of 'diversity-advantages', is a direct attack against the view of diversity as a direct source of conflict and disadvantages.

This particular vision of diversity, as far as I am aware, has never caught the attention of multicultural citizenship's or civic-national citizenship's theorists. In fact, it is probably the most powerful argument mobilized by intercultural citizenship's adherants to reinforce both diversity-awareness and diversity-recognition. This means seeing diversity as a public good, and the diversity-advantages public debate it generates can help to motivate people to accept diversity, considered now as being a source of development and a richness for people and society.[1] This does not mean that diversity becomes a simple commodity for private benefits. However, this trend exists. Today diversity is a fashionable word that helps to sell products that may still be viewed as exotic. Today the diversity-word is elsewhere and has even become a cliché for public marketing ('today we will celebrate the "diversity day"!'), a market good used even by cities' public authorities. A greater emphasis on interaction, bridging practices and the

---

[1] I develop this dimension of motivation further in Zapata-Barrero (2015b).

exchange of ideas can lead to a 'diversity dividend' of private/social economic benefits (Syrett and Sepulveda, 2011). In seeking to realize the diversity-dividend, city public promotors have pursued a number of different strategies, from the branding of cities as vibrant, multicultural/cosmopolitan locations to attract investors, tourists, events and high-skilled workers (Musterd and Murie, 2010; Rath, 2007) to the promotion of, for example, ethnic businesses (Ram and Jones, 2008), diaspora trading networks (Kitching et al., 2009; Kuznetsov and Sabel, 2006), ethnic quarters and festivals (Shaw, 2007). In contrast to this literature, the substantial argument I want to put forward is mostly concerned with how diversity can generate public benefits through the making of intercultural citizenship.

The guiding thread of this book has been that promoting a learning and socializing process through diversity-contacts can help to foster a public culture based on diversity-recognition and shared public spaces. Now, to close this rationale path, we will centre on the public benefits the practice of intercultural citizenship may produce. Here we change our perspective. We leave the domain of the conditions of intercultural citizenship that have oriented previous chapters and enter directly into a discussion of the outcomes of intercultural citizenship. In general terms, we are now heading to map the main public results of intercultural citizenship. In this way we can offer additional arguments for justifying the value of putting diverse people in contact in public spaces, and hence justify the social engineering mechanisms behind intercultural citizenship.

If we look at the Intercultural Cities programme of the Council of Europe (2011a), it incorporated a competitive call in March 2015 for cities to select the best practical initiatives on diversity advantage challenges. The way they define the diversity advantage is broad but it fits the focus we want to follow in this chapter perfectly: 'Recognising that diversity is not a threat – it can bring competitive benefits for businesses, organisations and communities if managed competently and in the spirit of inclusion', 'Embracing diversity is not a gimmick for the branding of a business, organisation or city but a philosophy of governance, management and decision making' (Council of Europe, 2015: 3).

The diversity-advantage approach of interculturalism (Wood and Landry, 2008)[2] certainly emerges assuming the economic development hypothesis leading the debate. Despite the seeming unanimity of intercultural theorists on

---

[2] The concept of diversity-advantage has been introduced by the UK think tank Comedia directed by Wood (2004), mainly inspired by Zachary's (2003) seminal work.

the merits of contacts, they probably differ (in terms of emphasizing differently, rather than opposing) concerning the kinds of outcomes intercultural citizenship aims to produce. We can even wonder whether there can be different kinds of specific strategies for different kinds of outcomes.

To better define this focus, a short discussion about what 'benefits' means may be helpful. What does 'benefit' mean? It is an advantage or profit gained from something or some situation in our case; a helpful or good effect, something that produces well-being. The etymology is quite explit; to do <'facere' good 'bene'>: 'to do goods', 'good deed'. The public benefit, then, is a public good for the collective, the society. This outcome gives sense to intercultural citizenship policies as an archetype of distributive policies aimed at ensuring proper distribution of opportunities among all the population. It is – properly speaking – a distributive public policy in terms of encouraging certain activities and refers to the provision of benefits to citizens, rather than a regulatory policy in the sense that even if it seeks to promote certain behaviours it does not have the compelling dimension a regulatory policy needs.

The meaning of public benefit we use is directly related to the fact that by fostering this policy there is a potential decrease in racism and xenophobia and an increase in the welfare of a society. The empirical problems are, however, highly recognized by public policy studies: social benefits, as such, cannot easily be quantified. A great amount of normative dimension needs to be articulated and evidenced by several studies. In section 1, I overview the literature pointing to the benefits diversity may produce when it is managed following intercultural citizenship. In section 2, I discuss antiracism and other related social effects. In section 3, I do the same with well-being and quality-of-life literature.

1. INTERCULTURAL CITIZENSHIP AS A MEDIATOR FOR LINKING DIVERSITY AND ADVANTGES: AN OVERVIEW

That diversity as a social asset is theoretically recognized and empirically demonstrated in many studies coming from business, workplace and labour relations, urban studies, education and social psychology. It has been brillanty summarized by Fainstein (2005: 4):

> Diversity attracts human capital, encourages innovation, and ensures fairness and equal access to a variety of groups. The competitive advantage of cities, and thus the most promising approach to attaining economic success, lies in enhancing diversity within the society, economic base, and built environment. Diversity and creativity work together to power innovation and economic growth.

Taking diversity as a driver for benefits, there is always the obvious assumption that this connection is not direct or automatic, but mediated. Thus, instead of concentrating on this connection we need to focus on what the positive or neutral or even negative mediators promoting benefits are. We take a large notion of benefits as an outcome related to the context that creates positive resources for those within this context. In this case the focus is that intercultural citizenship is one positive mediator than can produce a multiplicity of benefits depending on contextual conditions and the way contact is made. It is at this precise point that the argument that intercultural citizenship is social engineering becomes meaningful. Some studies have even predicted that close intercultural encounters, friendly, family and romantic, are the best type of intercultural contact to produce benefits and creativity (Gareis, 1995; Lu et al., 2017).

This particular conception of diversity as a potential benefit for society, and intercultural citizenship interpreted as a policy strategy to promote these advantages, basically have an individual and a socio-economic dimension. Intercultural citizenship sees individuals as holders of competences that need to be promoted. An immigrant has several added competences and skills in terms of social and cultural capital, such as language, culturally differentiated registers, cultural-particular worldviews and knowledge. At this individual level, we also know from the seminal influential work of Berry (2013) that interculturalism is seen as the most appropriate tool to promote creativity in society. This follows the interest in strengthening the distinctive assets of diversity-contacts, such as trust, mutual knowledge and prejudice reduction (Howarth and Andreouli, 2013).

From the socio-economic side, this diversity advantage approach comes from global business studies (Zachary, 2003), which focuses on the economic benefits of diversity. The private sector has led the way on this, evolving the idea that there is a 'business case for diversity' because diverse teams of people bring new skills and aptitudes, which can produce new processes and product innovations to advance competitiveness.

Although team-based structures in firms can contribute to the successful generation and implementation of ideas, dangers that are particular to cross-cultural teams remain. If the work in teams produces a climate of mistrust, threat and anxiety, it damages the innovation process (Bouncken et al., 2016). Gompers and Kovvali (2018) have recently examined the decisions of thousands of venture capitalists and tens of thousands of investments, and the evidence is clear: diversity significantly improves financial performance on measures such as profitable investments at the individual portfolio-company level and overall fund returns, and on the contrary, homogeneous teams have worse investment outcomes. This leads them to ask how to improve ethnic representation within a firm. Evidence from business studies suggests that there is a 'diversity advantage' that can provide opportunities. Diversifying a workforce introduces new skills and aptitudes, often leading to innovations, and provides access to new markets and a variety of cheaper goods. There is also evidence that a tolerant and diverse setting can attract wealth creators to a city. Finally, there are also traditional recognized studies suggesting that countries with high levels of diversity are better able to adapt to new technologies and ideas (Florida, 2011). Ashraf and Galor (2011) argue that what really propelled Europe and the New World's economic ascendancy was their relative openness to other cultures, which they measure in terms of greater or lesser geographical isolation. Their findings overwhelmingly suggest that cultural diversity and geographic openness matter significantly to economic development. Cultural diversity has a positive impact on economic development in the process of industrialization, from its inception through modern times. Empirical contrasted routes lead then to the same square: diverse teams are more productive and perform better; geographical openness and cultural diversity are not by-products but key drivers of economic progress. Indeed, one might even go so far as to suggest that they provide the motivating force of intellectual, technological and artistic evolution.

Diversity has become increasingly pertinent as a source of invention and innovation, as we have seen, but also as a resource for sustainable economic development. But again, this statement must be taken carefully, since the transformative dimension of interculturalism is not automatic. Reynolds (2017) signals, for instance, the challenges that must be met to ensure this transformative potential: colleagues from some cultures may be less likely to let their voices be heard; integration across diverse teams can be difficult in the face of prejudice or negative cultural stereotypes; professional communication can be misinterpreted or difficult to understand across languages and cultures; navigating visa requirements, employment laws, and the cost of accommodating workplace requirements can be difficult; different understandings of professional etiquette can cause confusion or offence; conflicting working styles across teams could create problems.

Applied to society, this basically means that diversity can be seen as a driver of social and economic development. This line of discussion connects with other studies that follow the traditional view of the economic benefits of immigration (Borjas, 1995). The link between diversity and economic performance is also contributing to the consolidation of intercultural citizenship (see Alesina and LaFerrara, 2005; Bellini et al., 2009; Janssens et al., 2009; Müller et al., 2011; Wagner, 2015). Yet a number of studies on the intercultural approach include discussions of the growth, productivity and employment impact of diversity (Khovanova-Rubicondo and Pinelli, 2012); of governance structures and processes (see, for instance, Zapata-Barrero, 2016b); of urban space planning (see, for instance, Wood, 2015); of housing and neighbourhood policies; and of security and policing policies. For urban studies, diversity-contact has even become a new planning orthodoxy (Fainstein, 2005; Vormann, 2015) and it is related to innovation, development and creative cities (Florida, 2002, 2005). The central message of Landry (2012), for instance, is that cities are changing dramatically in ways that amount to a paradigm shift. The dogma is that diverse cities offer scope for communication, new ideas and wealth creation. There is also a long tradition of the benefits of encounters, which we can consider within a sociology of diversity. Simmel (1950) for instance, already hailed everyday encounters with difference as crucial for the development of novel personalities.

The awareness that the key to giving some continuity and permanence to this intercultural citizenship must come from these evidence-based arguments has been there from the very beginning, knowing that probably most of the key legitimating problems of multicultural citizenship have their roots in these empirical shortcomings, and was first thought up in academia before properly being tested. However, this contextual concern has also been there from the very beginning (Lægaard, 2016).

At the personal level, we can reproduce the benefits of an intercultural classroom to the whole society. Interculturalism helps people become more empathetic and flexible, more collaborative with communities, it helps them to relate better with others. The following components are also allocated as individual assets: the recognition of the value of cultural diversity, the readiness for contact with others, the attitude towards mutual changes during such an inter-personal exchange (Chebotareva, 2015).

Even if there is still a recognition that representation in sport management remains very homogeneous (Dashper and Fletcher, 2013), there is a scholarly consensus that sports and leisure are good practice for intercultural encounters, where most public benefits of diversity interact and are maximized. In a stimulating article Frisby (2014) shows us how leisure could be a practice for interculturalism. Bringing together culturally diverse individuals through physical activity fosters intercultural citizenship. Blending of cultures through sport promotes diversity-contacts, whereby different people are encouraged to communicate with one another, and learn from one another. Gaspirini and Cometti (2010: 12) also show us how 'sport is a human activity resting on fundamental social, educational and cultural values. It is a factor making for integration, involvement in social life, tolerance, acceptance of differences and playing by the rules'. Sports clubs have unquestionably formed a vital link in the chain of encounter, catalyzing its members to share values, common rules and customs, and cement relations of complicity, solidarity or friendship (Gasparini and Cometti, 2010). Social inclusion is promoted by engaging in practices that reduce barriers, leverage resources responsibly, and are underpinned by an ethic of care. Sport is culture, and if we take culture in a broad sense, as artistic activities, there is a direct link between intercultural citizenship and cultural citizenship (Zapata-Barrero, 2016d). Culture is a fundamental communication channel; it can link children and parents, the young and seniors, and it can also foster inter-class relations. Through a cultural event people can share the same public space, and in this way awareness-raising of diversity and diversity-recognition may be subtly generated. Culture is the basic communication mediator for young people, and practised in the public space, where young people have a non-hierachical space of socialization, in contrast with schools and family, it can be an excellent framework for intercultural citizenship.

These several empirical arguments coming from a great number of studies and sectors show us that promoting diversity-contacts involves generating social relations that can have productive public benefits. In the remainder of this chapter, I will review some case studies directly targeting the most public benefits of intercultural citizenship.

2. ANTIRACISM, AGAINST XENOPHOBIA AND INTERCULTURALISM

Some of the key findings of the 'Diversity and Contact' (DivCon) Project (Schönwälder et al., 2016) are of interest to us, in particular the argument that has been put forward: in the context of diversities, only those who have diverse-social ties are less influenced by racism and other factors which threaten social cohesion. This is a strong argument for intercultural citizenship, when we know these ties exist among people from different backgrounds. Social ties, it appears, can effectively overcome the feeling of being threatened by diversity, and then enhance diversity-recognition and shared spaces, the two main pillars of intercultural citizenship. Within this trend of research there is also a similar argument, which we have already highlighted when speaking about transnational minds: namely, those people who have multiple and complex identities have more propensity to maintain social ties with people of different backgrounds. The assumption that empirical studies have demonstrated is that such positive feelings might contribute to the development of generalized trust, especially when strong ties occur in neighbourhood settings (Stolle et al., 2008). Clearly, there are also patterns of social interaction that are not necessarily linked to ethnicity and 'race', such as social status, age or education (Petermann and Schönwälder, 2014), that can have a multiplier effect when clustered by ethnicity and nationality. If this can happen socially, without policy intervention, when there is a policy narrative targeting a change of mind towards diversity, to dissipate people's initial fears and negative emotions, consolidated most of the time with prejudices and stereotypes, then the learning and socializing process put in place by the intercultural citizenship narrative seems to be more than justified.

These preliminary studies can be the base from which to explore a xenophobia-reduction hypothesis. Roughly speaking, the argument is that intercultural citizenship can contribute to reducing the space of anti-immigration populism and be a tool for anti-racism policies.[3] That is, in promoting contact, intercultural citizenship helps to reduce ethno-national narratives, racism, prejudice, false stereotypes and negative public opinions, which restrict reasons for contact between people from different diversity-categories. The operationalization of this hypothesis takes different levels of analysis. From a political party point of view, the hypothesis can mean that intercultural citizenship tends to reduce public space for political parties with clear national xenophobic narratives. From a public opinion perspective, it can also mean that once the intercultural citizenship is working, the negative attitudes towards diversity tend to also decrease. In addition, we know that some of the main discursive frameworks of xenophobia are social welfare, identity and security related (Helbling, 2012), which raises the point that multiculturalism, as it generates specific policies, contributes to in-group monoculturalism and could also be at the forefront of prejudices and rumours related to immigration that are directly hyper-emphasized by xenophobic parties. So probably the main argument that can consolidate intercultural citizenship is that universal policies can contribute to reducing the two main drivers of xenophobic narrative: specific policies increase public budgets for a 'privileged' cultural-differentiated group of people.

---

[3] The first time I defended this argument was in a discussion paper. See Zapata-Barrero (2011).

This anti-racist dimension of intercultural citizenship has been examined in depth by education studies. Gundara (2000) incorporates, for instance, the argument that intercultural education is a remedy for racism, xenophobia and anti-immigration rhetoric (Chapter 5: pp. 105–44), and that interculturalism is a strategy to build a common and shared value system (Chapter 7: pp. 145–60).[4] It has also been applied in policy studies only recently (Barn, 2012; Carr, 2016; Pinxten and Cornelis, 2002) and as a key strategic line by some national plans, such as the debated Irish one (Fanning, 2002), which seeks to foster positive local interculturalism to inform place-based anti-racism interventions. It even becomes more prominent today to explore this link given the context of rising radicalization in most xenophobic narratives. It is from this side that intercultural citizenship can be considered a tool for fighting against one of the main concerns in European countries today: extremism in all its forms, namely political and social xenophobia on the one hand and terrorist attacks by supremacists and Islamism on the other hand.

This probably explains why many programmes that are aimed at fighting rumours, prejudices and negative perceptions towards diversity are in expansion in Europe (see Council of Europe, 2014). This hypothesis is related to a line of thought seeking the conditions for reducing spaces of xenophobia and racism. This line of empirical arguments that intercultural citizenship can also help break stereotypes and xenophobia is also endorsed by intercultural communication studies. There the effectiveness of intercultural communication becomes visible when it is shown how it dispels myths, breaks down stereotypes, fosters more respect and acceptance, and builds more cooperative social relations diversity-categories. The scope of the intercultural communication perspective is really broad, but nonetheless important to highlight. It includes not only values, beliefs and practices, but also nonverbal communication, body language, eye contact, gestures, posture, dress, personal space, touch, compliments and silence (Samovar et al., 2015).

3. WELL-BEING, QUALITY OF LIFE, COHESION, HUMAN RIGHTS AND DEMOCRACY

Summarizing the results of different empirical studies on intercultural interaction, Chebotareva (2015) states that people feel tension in diversity-contacts when they perceive the situation as threatening their well-being. This is why the question of how different types of cultures (nationality, religion and ethnicity)

---

[4]See also Gundara (2005).

together influence the person's subjective well-being, in the context of diversity-related contact, becomes meaningful for intercultural citizenship.

In fact, we can see the relation in a circular fashion. The assumption is also that human well-being is facilitated by a sense of connectedness to other people. In this case, social cohesion is the most widely researched concept, which expresses this human connectedness in the civic and public realms (Bynner, 2016: 22). Local well-being has been measured across Europe through Eurobarometer 419 (European Commission, 2016) on *Quality of Life in European Cities*, which surveyed around 500 people in 79 European cities. Questions included the following: Is the presence of foreigners good for the city? Do the administrative services of the city help people efficiently? Generally speaking, can the public administration of the city be trusted? Do you feel safe in the city? Is it easy to find a job? (2016: 76–85). A recent report requested by the Intercultural Cities programme (ICC) (Migration Policy Group, 2017) has also shown how local intercultural policies still emerge as significant drivers behind local well-being and attitudes towards immigrants. This exploratory study highlights that people were more likely to report local well-being in cities with higher ICC index scores. It is also important to signal that we cannot have a linear causal view, since intersectionality may provide a better picture of reality, also inviting us to see the circularity of most of the correlations.

> The two could be linked to some third underlying cause; for example, wealthier cities may have stronger intercultural policies and higher reported levels of well-being. Or a causal relationship may exist in the opposite direction than expected; for example, only populations with high levels of well-being may be willing to support an intercultural approach. (Migration Policy Group, 2017: 5)

But even with these intersectional controls, the study strongly supports the argument that cities with stronger intercultural policies are significantly more likely to have populations that think foreigners are good for the city, services are trustworthy and the city is efficient, safe and good for finding jobs.

Now, there is also a growing interest in researching the main drivers of solidarity practices. This debate also belongs to a widespread concern about how interculturalism can foster trust, social capital. From different angles and perspectives, all belong to the same conceptual family of the traditional term of cohesion. For me, the basic efforts of these empirical studies are based on the common premise that cohesion can also be possible in heterogeneous societies, and then contribute to building a strong argument against those who still ground their xenophobic narratives on the assumption that cohesion is only possible in homogeneous societies (Portes and Vickstrom, 2011).

That intercultural citizenship can foster social inclusion means in practice that it can nurture positive bonding between people and help bridge the gaps that may arise when diverse cultural views intersect. All these dimensions constitute key elements of intercultural citizenship. Roughly speaking, cohesion means the action or fact of forming, and accepting to live in, shared spaces. It also means togetherness, interpersonal linkage and interrelatedness. It is the contrary to diversity which is always seen as a source of conflict: segregation, territorial separatedness, multiple institutions, differentiated rights and duty assignations, and even ignorance and indifference among cultures. In this sense, it is not the context of cultural diversity that leads to conflict so much as how diversity, including the social processes to which it gives rise, is understood and managed.

A cohesive society works towards the well-being of all its members, fights exclusion and marginalization, creates a sense of belonging, promotes trust, and offers its members the opportunity of upward social mobility (Organisation for Economic Co-operation and Development (OECD), 2011: 17). While the notion of 'social cohesion' is often used with different meanings, its constituent elements remain the same. According to one of the last OECD reports (2011) on cohesion, this can include concerns about (a) social inclusion or the process of improving the terms for individuals and groups to take part in society – it aims to empower poor and marginalized people to take advantage of rising global opportunities; (b) social capital or the resources that result from people cooperating together towards common ends; (c) social mobility or the ability of individuals or groups to move upwards or downwards in status based on wealth, occupation, education, or other social variables. The majority of policy-oriented studies recommend, again, intersectional analysis, in the sense that several diversity-categories can interact and constitute a factor of cohesion or not. In this sense, and again taking the 2011 OECD report as reference, intercultural citizenship policies centred on cohesion promotion recommend going beyond anti-discrimination measures and including a comprehensive set of social, employment, education and housing measures, to include Improvement of native-born citizens' perceptions of immigrants; preventing and reversing the social exclusion of immigrants; fostering positive bonding between immigrants and native people; promoting social mobility for immigrants by improving labour market mobility, facilitating entrepreneurship, better skills matching, and encouraging education.

To speak about well-being, quality of life, cohesion, belongs to an array of key concepts related to intercultural citizenship, such as democracy and human rights. These are also considered to be key parameters of interculturalism.

UNESCO (2009) goes a step further by arguing that to invest in intercultural dialogue is to invest in a democratic society, based on human rights and cohesion. This human rights approach is probably the basis of intercultural citizenship for most international and city-based policies (Berry, 2018: Evans and Weber, 2017). When the EU, for instance, incorporated interculturalism into its agenda, it immediately made it explicit that interculturalism is linked to European values such as human rights, democracy and a culture of peace and dialogue (Bekemans, 2012; Council of Europe, 2008; European Commission, 2008b; Vidmar-Horvat, 2012). The public benefits of being linked to the EU and intercultural citizenship are fed back in this case.

Throughout this book we have already highlighted in several chapters how Cantle's main argument, that interculturalism fosters community cohesion, is grounded on pragmatic devices, against territorial ethnic-based isolation, and the consequent lack of shared public space. That intercultural citizenship is a strategy that can transform the link between diversity and cohesion in positive rather than negative ways, as Putnam's work highlighted (2007), is corroborated by the evidence-based argument of numerous critical studies. Most of the empirical studies in Europe that have tested Putnam's thesis contest these findings and argue that social contact is not weakened by diversity. Again, intersectional studies are here illuminating. It is economic deprivation rather than diversity that has the most damaging effect, and this effect is mediated by mutual support and contact between neighbours (Bécares et al., 2011; Gesthuizen et al., 2009). Here again we should raise awareness of the importance of intersectional research in diversity studies (Lutz, 2015). The findings from most European studies suggest that economic deprivation 'drowns out' any negative effect of diversity on social capital, and that the issue is not lack of sociability in the neighbourhood but lack of access to resources such as employment, housing and welfare (Hooghe et al., 2009; Laurence, 2011; Letki, 2008). Therefore, a review of the literature linking diversity and poverty is likely to have a negative effect on trust in neighbours and attitudes towards the neighbourhood. However, negative attitudes do not necessarily affect everyday behaviours.

CONCLUDING ROADMAP: SUMMARIZING WHAT THE READER HAS FOUND IN THIS BOOK

The recent debate between multiculturalism and interculturalism probably illustrates that we are witnessing a process of policy-paradigm change. The role of a policy paradigm is to frame policy-making, and we cannot deny that intercultural citizenship has already attracted many cities and local policy makers from all over Europe and elsewhere. From the point of view of public acceptance, it has even reached a level of consensus between society, policies and politics that has not occurred with other paradigms, such as civic-nationalism and multiculturalism. The emergence of intercultural citizenship in Europe is directly related to the 'local turn' in migration and diversity studies (Zapata-Barrero et al., 2017), with pragmatic devises regarding the way to govern diversity.

The whole book has expressed a deliberate effort to engage the migration-related diversity debate towards a consideration of diversity as a public good, and then justify why intercultural citizenship is the most appropriate focus for raising awareness of this view as it allows the promotion of diversity as a public culture, a culture of diversity. In a few words, this book has been centred around answering the key question on how to govern diversity understood as a public good through diversity-contact promotion.

The development of the intercultural citizenship argument has been contextualized within the post-M era. The prefix 'post-' has been used in two senses: analytically, it has an obvious temporal dimension. It indicates that we are entering into a new historical context. Normatively it also means that we are experiencing a paradigm change, a policy turn in the way we have conducted diversity management. In this case 'post-' has basically been used to express the view that we need to go beyond the multicultural master narrative.

As a narrative, intercultural citizenship shapes a diversity approach and articulates a set of ideas that may help to develop a philosophical ideology, a political strategy, a policy mechanism, and even an epistemological methodology. It has a transformative engineering nature, and as such it tries to foster something that is valuable for people and can make the society develop its tools to domesticate the current historical path of globalization: the diversity that arises from the global movement of people. By its nature it is not an end in itself. It has been analysed in this book as a mediating function. Intercultural citizenship, then, has been fashioned as a policy strategy that may help to channel all the negative by-products of a dynamic of diversity that is spreading in society, without policy intervention. The development of socializing mechanisms for diversity-recognition and a culture of diversity, together with the promotion of diversity-encounters, diversity-interdependencies, diversity-interactions and diversity-solidarity practices, in shared public spaces, have also been at the core of the intercultural citizenship narrative that we have put forward. This intercultural citizenship philosophy has then been presented as a remedy to avoid the consequences of a poorly managed or simply unmanaged diversity, which still defines the same diversity category from the point of view of a homogeneous hegemonic national culture.

This lack of intercultural mindedness and diversity in public culture is probably one of the great shortcomings that we have nowadays in our liberal democratic societies. Such worries are not new in our history of the *longue durée*, to speak in Braudel's terms. Ordinary people have always had difficulty joining the main course of history without directly suffering its consequences in terms of injustice and inequality. Schönwälder et al. (2016: 2) remind us, for instance, that 'in some ways these discussions resemble debates about the consequences of urbanization around the turn of the twentieth century. At that time, the rapid development of large cities, driven by industrialization, was associated with a loss of community, a prediction that did not come true'. Social class has always been the main criterion for understanding the course of history. Today, even if social class remains an explanatory factor, with the reality of diversity it is often interlinked with race, ethnicity and culture, and also other categories of difference, such as gender, religion, sexual orientation, age and education. This makes a complex social and political cocktail with negative and positive potentialities.

We must then accept that diversity has a Janus face, which goes from extreme otherness to togetherness. We all know the negative side of migration-related diversity: social disturbances, racism, xenophobia, discrimination, inequality, unbalanced power relations, unethical treatment, human rights infringement, loss of traditional values, stereotypes, prejudices and lack of confidence, amongst others. Today all these categories can be perfectly encapsulated under the broad framework of 'social conflict'. We know less the positive side in terms of social benefits, that is to consider diversity as a public good.

In this sense, intercultural citizenship not only has a reactive dimension, as it can be viewed following a conflict-based approach and then understood as a mechanism to reduce the factors of diversity-related conflicts, but most importantly a proactive dimension, in terms of fostering creativity, new terms of cohesion, innovation, solidarity and economical/social performance. The key to grasp this mediator role, the transformative function and the engineering nature of interculturalism is to understand that the positive face cannot come ex-novo, it needs to be politically and socially enhanced.

This book has dealt with this mechanism. The main purpose, then, has been not only to theorize the need for intercultural citizenship, but to defend a particular vision of what is urgently needed if we want to counteract the devastating effects (and probably historical involution) that the dynamics of diversity can produce without public intervention. Interculturalism is a citizenship-making process. To speak about intercultural citizenship is first of all to speak about a learning and socializing process into a public culture of diversity. This basically means that there is a need to foster in all the spheres of our society something that is basic, but still pending: diversity-recognition and getting shared public spaces. These are the leitmotivs of intercultural and republican citizenship, which have direct structural transformative implications. The focus on shared spaces has the effect of not only changing our perspective on diversity, going from state to urban settings, but also invites us to directly explore diversity territorially, at the micro-level, at the level of streets and neighbourhood.

Likewise, and probably more substantially, it involves recognizing that there is nothing empirically grounded that tells us that political stability and social cohesion can only be reached with homogeneous societies. Finally, I have had the opportunity to argue that intercultural citizenship assumes not only diversity-representation (the presence of diversity in all the representative bodies of our society) and diversity-participation (the opportunity to be recognized as a political and social actor, and not only a passive individual), but basically diversity-contacts in all the realms of our everyday life. This is a need that even the liberal multicultural scholar W. Kymlicka recognizes, stating that 'we have multicultural states populated by citizens who have only minimal levels of intercultural interaction or knowledge' (2003: 155). He even continues claiming that '[W]e should encourage individuals to have the ability and desire to seek out interactions with the members of other groups, to have curiosity about the larger world, and to learn about the habits and beliefs of other peoples' (2003: 158).

We know from a long social psychological tradition that cultural learning can be defined as the acquisition of new information and understanding about the assumptions, beliefs, customs, norms, values or language of another culture (Lu et al., 2017). Such cultural learning allows both sides to recognize that different cultural scripts underlie the same surface behaviour and, as a result, to approach future situations with greater cognitive flexibility and complexity (Tadmor et al., 2012). We have insisted throughout these pages that intercultural citizenship enhances open-mindedness and – this is crucial – a predisposition to change one's own mind and views, to have multiple visions and perspectives, as a result of diversity-contact.

Diversity-recognition and sharing public spaces are paramount drivers of intercultural citizenship. They assume that we need to change current parameters of diversity interpretation. The new intercultural citizenship paradigm needs to break down the epistemological barriers of diversity management, namely the theoretical frameworks of Unity/Diversity and Majority/Minority that govern most diversity views. Diversity can no longer be used as a euphemism of 'others-against-us', which maintains the inequalities and unbalanced power relations based on diversity instead of reducing them.

Viewed in such a way, intercultural citizenship can be perfectly understood as a new spirit in migration and ethnic studies, which takes its legitimacy from all the positive by-products of diversity-contact. My purpose with this book, then, has been to draw up this intercultural citizenship agenda. To do this, I have necessarily been forced to face the master narrative that has governed the diversity debate these past two decades: multiculturalism. This is why I have placed intercultural citizenship within this scholarly diversity context. I clearly state the similarities and differences it has, without any ambition to enter into a more critical discussion on multiculturalism in a, for me, unfruitful debate about who is best and worst. As in the title of one of my most recent works (Zapata-Barrero, 2018a), multiculturalism and interculturalism are alongside, but separate paradigms. This separateness must not be interpreted in conflictive terms but in complementary ones. I have also had more opportunity to go into details along this argument. But it is also true that, as an emerging policy paradigm, interculturalism needs, in this first historical phase, to find a place for itself, and the only way to do this is to focus more on the differences than on the similarities. Hence, I have opted to place the intercultural citizenship debate within what I have termed the post-M era. It is within this historical context that I have argued that intercultural citizenship offers new interpretative maps and a different way of zooming in/out of the diversity dynamics. It is from this angle that I have proposed how intercultural citizenship can be a new way to reboot European identity: it has a republican citizenship background, a different epistemology and a mainstreaming policy purpose; it includes from the very beginning national citizens as a target population; and probably more importantly, it can be clustered to the consolidated patterns of super-diversity, cosmopolitanism and transnationalism. Only policy practices and outcomes will tell us whether this emerging policy paradigm in the migration and diversity agenda has come here to stay or whether it has just been a short wave that has not managed to offer us the much-needed cordon sanitaire to prevent whatever form of extremism, be it supremacist, Islamist, or against-diversity populist ideology that threatens our liberal democracies.

REFERENCES

Abdallah-Pretceille, M. (2006) Interculturalism as a paradigm for thinking about diversity, *Intercultural Education*, 17(5): 475–83.

Agyeman, J. (2017) Interculturally inclusive spaces as just environments, *Items. Social Science Research Council*. Available at: https://items.ssrc.org/just-environments/interculturally-inclusive-spaces-as-just-environments/

Alesina, A. and LaFerrara, E. (2005) Ethnic diversity and economic performance, *Journal of Economic Literature*, 43(3): 762–800.

Allport, G.W. (1954) *The Nature of Prejudice*. Cambridge: Addison-Wesley.

Amin, A. (2002) Ethnicity and the multicultural city: Living with diversity, *Environment and Planning A*, 34(6): 959–80.

Amin, A. (2009) Collective culture and urban public space, *City*, 12(1): 5–24.

Antonsich, M. (2008) The narration of Europe in "National" and "Post-national" terms, *European Journal of Social Theory*, 11(4): 505–22.

Antonsich, M. (2016) Interculturalism versus multiculturalism: The Cantle–Modood debate, *Ethnicities*, 16(3): 470–93.

Ashraf, Q. and Galor, O. (2011) *Cultural Diversity, Geographical Isolation, and the Origin of the Wealth of Nations*. NBER Working Papers 17640, National Bureau of Economic Research, Inc.

Bagwell, S., Evans, G., Witting, A. and Worpole, K. (2012) *Public Space Management: Report to the Intercultural Cities Research Programme*. Cities Institute, London Metropolitan University. Available at: https://rm.coe.int/CoERMPublicCommonSearchServices/Display DCTMContent?documentId=09000016803009c0

Banting, K. and Kymlicka, W. (2006) *Multiculturalism and the Welfare State: Recognition and Redistribution in Contemporary Democracies*. Oxford: Oxford University Press.

Banting, K. and Kymlicka, W. (2013) Is there really a retreat from multiculturalism policies? New evidence from the multiculturalism policy index, *Comparative European Politics*, 11(5): 577–98.

Banting, K. and Kymlicka, W. (2015) *The Political Sources of Solidarity in Diverse Societies*. Robert Schuman Centre for Advanced Studies (RSCAS) Working Papers 73. Available at: https://cadmus.eui.eu/bitstream/handle/1814/37235/RSCAS_2015_73.pdf;sequence=1

Barrett, M. (ed.) (2013) *Interculturalism and Multiculturalism: Similarities and Differences*. Strasbourg: Council of Europe.

Barry, B. (2001) *Culture and Identity: An Egalitarian Critique of Multiculturalism*. Hoboken, NJ: Wiley.

REFERENCES

Barn, R. (2012). Interculturalism in Europe: Fact, fad or fiction – The deconstruction of a theoretical idea, In Farrar, M. et al. (eds) *Debating Multiculturalism 1*. In *Debating Multiculturalism* London: Dialogue Society.

Basch, L., Glick Schiller, N. and Szanton Blanc, C. (1994) *Nations Unbound: Transnational Projects, Postcolonial Predicaments and Deterritorialized Nation-States*. Amsterdam: Gordon and Breach.

Bauböck, R. (1997) *Citizenship and National Identities in the European Union*. Cambridge, MA: Harvard Law School.

Bauböck, R. (ed.) (2019) *Debating European Citizenship*. IMISCOE Research Series. Cham: Springer.

Bauböck, R. and Joppke, C. (eds) (2010) *How Liberal are Citizenship Tests?* EUI Working Paper, RSCAS, 41. Available at: https://hdl.handle.net/1814/13956

Bécares, L., Stafford, M., Laurence, J. and Nazroo, J. (2011) Composition, concentration and deprivation: Exploring their association with social cohesion among different ethnic groups in the UK, *Urban Studies*, 48(13): 2771–87.

Beck, U. and Grande, E. (2014) *Cosmopolitan Europe*. Cambridge: Polity Press.

Beck, U. and Sznaider, N. (2006) Unpacking cosmopolitanism for the social sciences: A research agenda, *The British Journal of Sociology*, 57(1): 1–23.

Becker, M.A. (2004) Managing diversity in the European Union: Inclusive European citizenship and third-country nationals, *Yale Human Rights and Development Law Journal*, 7(1): 132–83. Available at: https://digitalcommons.law.yale.edu/yhrdlj/vol7/iss1/5

Bekemans, L. (2012) *Intercultural Dialogue and Multi-level Governance in Europe: A Human Rights Based Approach*. Brussels: P.I.E. Peter Lang.

Bellini, E., Pinelli, D. and Ottaviano, G.I.P. (2009) Diversity, cities and economic development, in M.D. Janssens, D. Pinelli, D.C. Reymen and S. Wallman (eds), *Sustainable Cities: Diversity, Economic Growth, Social Cohesion*. Cheltenham: Edward Elgar Publishing Limited, pp. 44–75.

Bennett, T. (2001) *Differing Diversities: Transversal Study on the Theme of Cultural Policy and Cultural Diversity*. Strasbourg: Council of Europe

Berry, J.W. (2013) Intercultural relations in plural societies, in S. Guo and L. Wong (eds), *Revisiting Multiculturalism in Canada*. Rotterdam: Sense Publisher, pp. 37–49.

Berry, S.E. (2018) Aligning interculturalism with international human rights law: "Living together" without assimilation, *Human Rights Law Review*, 18(3): 441–71.

Bloemraad, I. and Wright, M. (2014) Utter failure or unity out of diversity? Debating and evaluating policies of multiculturalism, *International Migration Review*, 48(1): 292–334.

Blommaert, J. and Verschueren, J. (1998) *Debating Diversity: Analyzing the Discourse of Tolerance*. London: Routledge.

Bloomfield, J. and Bianchini, F. (2001) Cultural citizenship and urban governance in Western Europe, in N. Stevenson (ed.), *Culture and Citizenship*. London: Sage, pp. 99–123.

Bloomfield, J. and Bianchini, F. (2004) *Planning for the Intercultural City*. Stroud: Comedia.

Blumer, H. (1969). *Symbolic Interactionism: Perspective and Method*. Englewood Cliffs, N.J: Prentice-Hall.

Boccagni, P. (2015) The difference diversity makes: A principle, a lens, an empirical attribute for majority-minority relations, in T. Matejskova and M. Antonsich (eds), *Governing through Diversity: Migration Societies in Post-Multiculturalist Times*. London: Palgrave Macmillan, pp. 21–38.
Borjas, G. (1995) The economic benefits of immigration, *Journal of Economic Perspectives*, 9(2): 3–22.
Borkert, M., Bosswick, W., Heckmann, F. and Lüken-Klaßen, D. (2007) *Local Integration Policies for Migrants in Europe*. Luxembourg: Official Publications European Communities VIII.
Bouchard, G. (2011) What is interculturalism?, *McGill Law Journal* 56(2): 435–68.
Bouchard, G. (2012) *L'interculturalisme: Un point de vue québécois*. Montréal: Éditions du boreal.
Bouchard, G. (2015) *Interculturalism: A View from Quebec*. Toronto: University of Toronto Press.
Bouchard, G. and Taylor, C. (2008) *Bouchard–Taylor Report: Building the Future – A Time for Reconciliation*. Royal Commission, Quebec: Gouvernement du Quebec.
Boucher, F. and Maclure, J. (2018) Moving the debate forward: Interculturalism's contribution to multiculturalism, *Comparative Migration Studies*, 6(1): 1–10.
Bouncken, R., Brem, A. and Kraus, S. (2016) Multi-cultural teams as sources for creativity and innovation: The role of cultural diversity on team performance, *International Journal of Innovation Management*, 20(1): 1–34.
Bourdieu, P. (1979) Les trois etats du capital culturel, *Actes de la Recherche en Sciences Sociales*, 30: 3–6.
Bourdieu, P. (1984) *La distinction: a social critique of the judgement of taste*. Cambridge: MA: Harvard University Press.
Bradley, W. (2013) *Is There a Post-Multiculturalism?* Working paper series studies on multicultural societies No. 19, Afrasian Research Centre, Ryukoku University.
Brecknock, R., Caust, M., Howell, A. and Landry, C. (2007) Knowing lewisham, Bournes Green: Comedia. Available at: www.coe.int/t/dg4/cultureheritage/culture/cities/Publication/ Lewisham.pdf
Brewer, M.B. and Pierce, K.P. (2005) Social identity complexity and outgroup tolerance, *Personality and Social Psychology Bulletin*, 31(3): 428–38.
Brubaker, R. (2002) Ethnicity without groups, *European Journal of Sociology*, 43(2): 163–89.
Brubaker, R. (2012) Interview on 'diversity' conducted by F. Meissner. Available at: www.mmg.mpg.de/en/diversity-interviews/brubaker/
Bruter, M. (2005) *Citizens of Europe? The Emergence of a Mass European Identity*. London: Palgrave Macmillan.
Bynner, C. (2016) Towards an intercultural approach to social cohesion, in C. Braedel-Kühner and A.P. Müller (eds), *Re-thinking Diversity – Multiple Approaches in Theory, Media, Communities, and Managerial Practice*. Wiesbaden: Springer, pp. 21–34.
Byram, M. (2011) Intercultural citizenship from an internationalist perspective, *Journal of the NUS Teaching Academy*, 1(1): 10–20.
Calhoun, C.J. (ed.) (1992) *Habermas and the Public Sphere*. Cambridge, MA: MIT Press.

Cameron, D. (2011) David Cameron speech on radicalisation and Islamic extremism, *New Statesman*, Munich, 5 February, full transcript: Available at: www.newstatesman.com/blogs/the-staggers/2011/02/terrorism-islam-ideology

Cantle, T. (2001) *Community Cohesion: Report of the Independent Review Team – The 'Cantle Report'*. London: Home Office.

Cantle, T. (2008) *Community Cohesion: A New Framework for Race and Diversity*. Basingstoke: Palgrave Macmillan.

Cantle, T. (2012) *Interculturalism: The New Era of Cohesion and Diversity*. London: Palgrave Macmillan.

Caponio, T. and Borkert, M. (eds) (2010) *The Local Dimension of Migration Policymaking*. Amsterdam: Amsterdam University Press.

Caponio, T. and Donatiello, D. (2017) Intercultural policy in times of crisis: Theory and practice in the case of Turin, Italy, *Comparative Migration Studies*, 5(13).

Caponio, T. and Ricucci, R. (2015) Interculturalism: A policy instrument supporting social inclusion?, in R. Zapata-Barrero (ed.), *Interculturalism in Cities*. Cheltenham: Edward Elgar Publishing, pp. 20–34.

Caponio, T. Scholten, P. and Zapata-Barrero, R. (eds) (2018) *The Routledge Handbook of the Governance of Migration and Diversity in Cities*. London: Routledge.

Carr, J. (2016) *Experiences of Islamophobia: Living with Racism in the Neoliberal Era*. Abingdon and New York: Routledge.

Carr, S., Francis, M., Rivlin, L.G. and Stone, A.M. (1993). *Public Space*. Cambridge: Cambridge University Press.

Castells, M. (1999) *The Information Age: Economy, Society, and Culture, vol. 1: The Rise of the Network Society*. Oxford: Wiley-Blackwell.

Castiglione, D. (2009) Political identity in a community of strangers, in J. Checkel and P. Katzenstein (eds), *European Identity*. Cambridge: Cambridge University Press, pp. 29–51.

Castles, S. (2016) Migration and Community Formation under Conditions of Globalisation, in P. Kivisto (ed.) *Incorporating diversity: Rethinking assimilation in a multicultural age*. New York: Routledge, pp. 277–298.

Catarci, M. and Fiorucci, M. (2016) *Intercultural Education in the European Context: Theories, Experiences, Challenges*. London: Routledge.

Chebotareva, E. (2015) Life satisfaction and intercultural tolerance interrelations in different cultures, *European Journal of Social Sciences, Education and Research*, 2(4): 167–78.

Chopin, T. (2015) *Euroscepticism and Europhobia: The Threat of Populism*. European Issue No. 375, Fondation Robert Schuman. Available at: www.robert-schuman.eu/en/european-issues/0375-euroscepticism-and-europhobia-europe-under-the-test-of-populism

Cinalli, M. and Giugni, M. (2013) Public discourses about Muslims and Islam in Europe, *Ethnicities*, 13(2): 131–46.

Citrin, J. and Sides, I. (2004) Can there be Europe without Europeans? Problems of identity in a multinational community, in R. Herrmann, T. Risse and M.B. Brewer (eds), *Identities in Europe and the Institutions oj the European Union*. Lanham, MD: Rowman & Littlefield.

Collet, E. and Petrovic, M. (2014) *The Future of Immigrant Integration in Europe: Mainstreaming Approaches for Inclusion*. Brussels: Migration Policy Institute.

Collins, F.L. (2012) Transnational mobilities and urban spatialities: Notes from the Asia Pacific, *Progress in Human Geography*, 36(3): 316–35.

Comedia (2010) *Helsinki is an Open and Intercultural City*. Stroud: Comedia.

Council of Europe (2008) *White Paper on Intercultural Dialogue 'Living Together as Equals in Dignity.'* Strasbourg: Council of Europe.

Council of Europe (2011a) *Intercultural Cities*. Strasbourg: Council of Europe. Available at: www.coe.int/t/dg4/ cultureheritage/culture/cities/Index/default_en.asp

Council of Europe (2011b) *Living Together – Combining Diversity and Freedom in 21st Century Europe*. Strasbourg: Council of Europe. Available at: www.coe.int/t/dg4/highereducation/2011/KYIV%20WEBSITE/Report%20on%20diversity.pdf

Council of Europe (2014) *Communication for Integration: Antirumours Networks for Diversity*. Strasbourg: Council of Europe. Available at: www.pjp-eu.coe.int/en/web/c4i

Council of Europe (2015) *Diversity Advantge Challenge*. Strasbourg: Council of Europe. Available at: https://edoc.coe.int/en/living-together-diversity-and-freedom-in-europe/6555-diversity-advantage-challenge-selected-initiatives.html

Crepaz, M. (2006) If you are my brother, I may give you a dime! Public opinion on multiculturalism, trust and the welfare state, in K. Banting and W. Kymlicka (eds), *Multiculturalism and the Welfare State: Recognition and Redistribution in Contemporary Democracies*. Oxford: Oxford University Press, pp. 90–120.

Crowder, G. (2013) *Theories of Multiculturalism: An Introduction*. Oxford: Polity.

Crul, M., Schneider, J. and Lelie, F. (2012) *The European Second Generation Compared: Does the Integration Context Matter?* Amsterdam: Amsterdam University Press.

Daily Mail Reporter (2011) Nicolas Sarkozy joins David Cameron and Angela Merkel view that multiculturalism has failed. *Daily Mail*. Available at: www.dailymail.co.uk/news/article-1355961/Nicolas-Sarkozy-joins-David-Cameron-Angela-Merkel-view-multiculturalism-failed.html

Dashper, K. and Fletcher, T. (2013) Introduction: Diversity, equity and inclusion in sport and leisure, *Sport in Society*, 16(10): 1227–32.

Delafenetre, D. G. (1997) Interculturalism, multiracialism and transculturalism: Australian and Canadian experiences in the 1990s, *Nationalism and Ethnic Politics*, 3(1): 89–110.

Deutsch, K.W. (1966) *Nationalism and Social Communication: An Inquiry into the Foundations of Nationality*. Cambridge, MA: MIT Press.

Dines, N. and Cattell, V. with Gesler, W. and Curtis, S. (2006) *Public Spaces, Social Relations and Well-being in East London*. Bristol: The Policy Press.

Dobbernack, J. and Modood, T. (eds) (2013) *Tolerance, Intolerance and Respect. Hard to Accept?* London: Palgrave Macmillan.

Ecotec (2009) *Evaluation of the European Year of Intercultural Dialogue 2008 Final Report*. Birmingham: Ecotec. Available at: https://ec.europa.eu/culture/sites/culture/files/intercultural-dialogue-year-evaluation-2009_en.pdf

ECRI (European Commission against Racism and Intolerance) (2016) *Annual Report 2015*. Strasbourg: European Commission.

Eurocities (2009) *Intercultural Cities – A Journey through 23 European Cities*. Brussels: Council of Europe.

European Commission (2008a) *Intercultural Dialogue in Europe*. Available at: https://ec.europa.eu/culture/policy/strategic-framework/intercultural-dialogue_en.htm

European Commission (2008b) *Highlights of the European Year of Intercultural Dialogue*. Available at: https://eur-lex.europa.eu/legal-content/EN/TXT/?uri=URISERV%3Al29017

European Commission (2010) European Ministerial Conference on Integration, Zaragoza, 15–16 April. Available at: https://ec.europa.eu/migrant-integration/librarydoc/declaration-of-the-european-ministerial-conference-on-integration-zaragoza-15-16-april-2010

European Commission (2015) *Recommendation CM/Rec(2015)1 of the Committee of Ministers to Member States on intercultural integration*. (Adopted by the Committee of Ministers on 21 January 2015 at the 1217th meeting of the Ministers' Deputies). Available at: https://search.coe.int/cm/Pages/result_details.aspx?ObjectID=09000016805c471f

European Commission (2016) *Quality of Life in European Cities 2015, Flash Eurobarometer 419*. Luxembourg: European Union.

European Year of Intercultural Dialogue (2008) *Local government and interculturalism: The contribution of the Greek local authorities to the intercultural dialogue today*. Ministry of Interior and Ministry of Foreign Affairs, Hellenic Republic. Available at: https://ec.europa.eu/citizenship/pdf/doc891_en.pdf

Evans, M.D. and Weber, A. (2017) *Council of Europe Manuals: Human Rights in Culturally Diverse Societies*. Leiden: Nijhoff.

Fainstein, S. (2005) Cities and diversity: Should we want it? Can we plan for it?, *Urban Affairs Review*, 41(1): 3–19.

Faist, T., Fauser, M. and Reisenauer, E. (2013) *Transnational Migration*. Cambridge: Polity Press.

Fanning, B. (2002) *Racism and Social Change in the Republic of Ireland*. Manchester: Manchester University Press.

Favell, A. (2014) *Immigration, Integration and Mobility: New Agendas in Migration Studies*. Colchester: ECPR Press.

Favell, A. and Recchi, E. (eds) (2009) *Pioneers of European Integration: Citizenship and Mobility in the EU*. Cheltenham: Edward Elgar.

Festenstein, M. (2005) *Negotiating Diversity: Culture, Deliberation, Trust*. Cambridge: Polity.

Fligstein, N. (2010) *Euroclash: The EU, European Identity, and the Future of Europe*. Oxford: Oxford University Press.

Florida, R. (2002) *The Rise of the Creative Class*. New York: Basic Books.

Florida, R. (2005) *Cities and the Creative Classes*. New York: Routledge.

Florida, R. (2011) How diversity leads to economic growth, *CityLab*, 12 December. Available at: www.citylab.com/life/2011/12/diversity-leads-to-economic-growth/687/

Forbes, H.D. (1997) *Ethnic Conflict: Commerce, Culture, and the Contact Hypothesis*. New Haven, CT: Yale University Press.

Frazer, N. and Honneth, A. (2003) *Redistribution or Recognition? A Political-Philosophical Exchange*. London: Verso Books.

Friedrich, K.J. (1972) *Tradition and Authority*. London: Macmillan.

Frisby, W. (2014) Moving from multiculturalism to interculturalism through leisure, *Annals of Leisure Research*, 17(4): 354–58.

Gaertner, S.L., Dovidio, J.F., Anastasio, P.A., Bachman, B.A. and Rust, M.C. (1993) The common ingroup identity model: Recategorization and the reduction of intergroup bias, *European Review of Social Psychology*, 4(1): 1–26.

Gagnon, A. and Iacovino, R. (2016) Interculturalism and multiculturalism: Similarities and differences', in N. Meer, T. Modood and R. Zapata-Barrero (eds), *Multiculturalism and Interculturalism: Debating the Dividing Lines*. Edinburgh: Edinburgh University Press, pp. 104–32.

Galanakis, M. (2013) Intercultural public spaces in multicultural Toronto, *Canadian Journal of Urban Research*, 22(1): 67–89.

Garau, P. (2014) *Public Space: A Strategy for Achieving the Equitable City*. Durban: UCLG Committee on Urban Strategic Planning.

Gareis, E. (1995) *Intercultural Friendship: A Qualitative Study*. Lanham, MD: University Press of America.

Gasparini, W. and Cometti, A. (2010) *Sport Facing the Test of Cultural Diversity: Integration and Intercultural Dialogue in Europe, Analysis and Practical Examples*. Strasbourg: Council of Europe.

Geddes, A. (2003) *The Politics of Migration and Immigration in Europe*. London: Sage.

Gehl, J. (2011) *Life Between Buildings: Using Public Space* (J. Koch, Trans.). Washington, DC: Island Press.

Gehl, J. and Matan, A. (2009) Two perspectives on public spaces, *Building Research and Information*, 37(1): 106–9.

Gehl, J. and Rogers, L.R. (2010) *Cities for People*. Washington, DC: Island Press.

Gesthuizen, M., van der Meer, T. and Scheepers, P. (2009) Ethnic diversity and social capital in Europe: Tests of Putnam's thesis in European countries, *Scandinavian Political Studies*, 32(2): 121–42.

Glick Schiller, N. (2011) Transnationality and the city, in G. Bridge and S. Watson (eds), *The New Blackwell Companion to the City*. Oxford: Wiley-Blackwell. pp. 179–92.

Glick Schiller, N. and Irving, A. (2017) *Whose Cosmopolitanism? Critical Perspectives, Relationalities and Discontents*. New York: Berghahn Books.

Gompers, P. and Kovvali, S. (2018) The other diversity dividend, *Harvard Business Review*, 96(4): 72–7.

Goodhart, D. (2004) Too diverse: Is Britain becoming too diverse to sustain the mutual obligations behind a good society and the welfare state?, *Prospects Magazine*. Available at: www.prospectmagazine.co.uk/magazine/too-diverse-david-goodhart-multiculturalism-britain-immigration-globalisation

Goodman, S. (2012) Measurement and interpretation issues in civic integration studies: A rejoinder, *Journal of Ethnic and Migration Studies*, 38(1): 173–86.

Gozdecka, D.A., Ercan, S.A. and Kmak, M. (2014) From multiculturalism to post-multiculturalism: Trends and paradoxes, *Journal of Sociology*, 50(1): 51–64.

Gruescu, S. and Menne, V. (2010) *Bridging Differences: What Communities and Government Can Do to Foster Social Capital*. London: The Social Market Foundation.

Guidikova, I. (2015) Intercultural integration: A new paradigm for managing diversity as an advantage, in R. Zapata-Barrero (ed.), *Interculturalism in Cities: Concept, Policy and Implementation*. Cheltenham: Edward Elgar Publishing, pp. 136–51.

Gundara, J.S. (2000) *Interculturalism, Education and Inclusion*. London: Sage.

Gundara, J.S. (2005) Racism and intercultural issues in Urban Europe, in R. Pinxten and E. Preckler (eds), *Racism in Metropolitan Areas*. New York and Oxford: Berghahn Books, pp. 113–26.

Gundara, J.S. and Jacobs, S. (eds) (2000) *Intercultural Europe: Diversity and Social Policy*. Aldershot: Ashgate.

Gundara, J.S. and Portera, A. (2008) Theoretical reflections on intercultural education, *Intercultural Education*, 19(6): 463–68.

Habermas, J. (1991) *The Structural Transformation of the Public Sphere: An Inquiry into a Category of Bourgeois Society*. Cambridge, MA: MIT Press.

Hadj Abdou L. and Geddes, A. (2017) Managing superdiversity? Examining the intercultural policy turn in Europe, *Policy and Politics*, 45(4): 493–510.

Hall, P. (1993) Policy paradigms, social learning, and the state: The case of economic policymaking in britain, *Comparative Politics*, 25(3): 275–96.

Hall, S. (2000) Conclusion: The multicultural question, in B. Hesse (ed.), *Unsettled Multiculturalisms: Diasporas, Entanglements, Transruptions*. London: Zed Books, pp. 209–241.

Hall, S. (2012) *City, Street and Citizen: The Measure of the Ordinary*. London: Routledge.

Hampshire, J. (2013) *The Politics of Immigration: Contradictions of the Liberal State*. Cambridge: Polity Press.

Helbling, M. (ed.) (2012) *Islamophobia in Western Europe and North America*. London: Routledge/Taylor and Francis.

Hellgren, Zenia (2018) Class, race – and place: Immigrants' self-perceptions on inclusion, belonging and opportunities in Stockholm and Barcelona, *Ethnic and Racial Studies*. DOI: 10.1080/01419870.2018.1532095

Herrmann, R.K., Risse, T. and Brewer, M.B. (eds) (2004) *Transnational Identities: Becoming European in the EU*. Lanham, MD: Rowman & Littlefield.

Hewstone, M. (2015) Consequences of diversity for social cohesion and prejudice: The missing dimension of intergroup contact, *Journal of Social Issues*, 71(2): 417–38.

Hogan, J. and Howlett, M. (eds) (2015) *Policy Paradigms in Theory and Practice*. Basingstoke: Palgrave Macmillan.

Honohan, I. (2017) Liberal and republican conceptions of citizenship, in Schachar, A., Bauböck, R., Bloemraad, I. and Vink, M. (eds), *The Oxford Handbook of Citizenship*. Oxford University Press, pp. 83–106.

Hooghe, M., Reeskens, T., Stolle, D. and Trappers, A. (2009) Ethnic diversity and generalized trust in Europe, *Comparative Political Studies*, 42(2): 198–223.

Howarth, C. and Andreouli, E. (2013) *Has Multiculturalism Failed? The Importance of Lay Knowledge and Everyday Practice*. Institute of Social Psychology Research Paper, The London School of Economics and Political Science Publications.

Hussain, A., Law, B. and Haq, T. (2006) *Engagement with Culture: From Diversity to Interculturalism*. Leicester: University of Leicester, Vaughan Papers 41.

Isin, E.F. and Turner, B.S. (eds) (2002) *Handbook of Citizenship Studies*. London: Sage.

Iveson, K. (2007) *Publics and the City*. Oxford: Blackwell.

Jacobs, D. and Rea, A. (2007) The end of national models? Integration courses and citizenship trajectories inEurope, *International Journal on Multicultural Societies*, 9: 264–83.

Janssens, M.D., Pinelli, D., Reymen, D.C. and Wallman, S. (eds) (2009) *Sustainable Cities: Diversity, Economic Growth, Social Cohesion*. Cheltenham: Edward Elgar.

Joppke, C. (2004) The retreat of multiculturalism in the liberal state: Theory and policy, *British Journal of Sociology*, 55(2): 237–57.

Joppke, C. (2007) Beyond national models: Civic integration policies for immigrants in Western Europe, *West European Politics*, 30(1): 1–22.

Joppke, C. (2008) Immigration and the identity of citizenship: The paradox of universalism, *Citizenship Studies*, 12(6): 533–46.

Kastoryano, R. (ed.) (2009) *An Identity for Europe: The Relevance of Multiculturalism in EU Construction*. New York: Palgrave Macmillan.

Kastoryano, R. (2016) Vers un nationalisme transnational: redéfinir la nation, le nationalisme et le territoire, *Revue française de science politique*, 56(4): 533–53.

Khovanova-Rubicondo, K. and Pinelli, D. (2012) *Evidence of the Economic and Social Advantages of Intercultural Cities Approach*. Council of Europe. Available at: https://rm.coe.int/1680492f80

Kihato, C.W., Massoumi, M., Ruble, B.A., Subiros, P. and Garland, A.M. (eds) (2010) *Urban Diversity: Space, Culture, and Inclusive Pluralism in Cities Worldwide*. Baltimore, MD: Woodrow Wilson Center Press with Johns Hopkins University Press.

King, D. (2005) Facing the future: America's post-multiculturalist trajectory, *Social Policy and Administration*, 39(2): 116–29.

Kitching, J., Smallbone, D. and Athayde, R. (2009) Ethnic diasporas and business competitiveness: Minority-owned enterprises in London, *Journal of Ethnic and Migration Studies*, 35(4): 689–705.

Knapp, C. (2007) *8 Lessons to Promote Diversity in Public Places*. Project for Public Spaces. Available at: www.pps.org/article/diversityinpublicspaces

Kuhn, T. (2015) *Experiencing European Integration: Transnational Lives and European Identity*. Oxford: Oxford University Press.

Kuznetsov, Y. and Sabel, C. (2006) International migration of talent, diaspora networks and development: Overview of main issues, in Y. Kuznetsov (ed.) *Diaspora Networks and the International Migration of Skills*. Washington, DC: World Bank Institute, pp. 3–20.

Kymlicka, W. (1995) *Multiculturalism: A Liberal View of Minority Rights*. Oxford: Oxford University Press.

Kymlicka, W. (2003) Multicultural states and intercultural citizens, *Theory and Research in Education*, 1(2): 147–69.

Kymlicka, W. (2010) The rise and fall of multiculturalism? New debates on inclusion and accommodation in diverse societies, *International Social Science Journal*, 61(199): 97–112.

Kymlicka, W. (2015) The essentialist critique of multiculturalism: Theories, policies, ethos, in V. Uberoi and T. Modood (eds), *Multiculturalism Rethought: Interpretations, Dilemmas and New Directions*. Edinburgh: Edinburgh University Press, pp. 209–49.

Kymlicka, W. (2016a) Solidarity in diverse societies: Beyond neoliberal multiculturalism and welfare chauvinism, *Comparative Migration Studies*, 3(17): 2–19.

Kymlicka, W. (2016b) Defending diversity in an era of populism: Multiculturalism and interculturalism compared, in N. Meer, T. Modood and R. Zapata-Barrero (eds), *Interculturalism and Multiculturalism: Debating the Dividing Lines*. Edinburgh: Edinburgh University Press, pp. 158–77.

Labelle, M. and Rocher, F. (2009) Immigration, integration and citizenship policies in Canada and Quebec, in R. Zapata-Barrero (ed.), *Immigration and Self-Government of Minority Nations*. Bruxelles: Peter Lang, Collection Diversitas: 57–85.

Labelle, M. and Salée, D. (2001) Immigrant and minority representations of citizenship in Quebec, in T.A. Aleinikoff and D.B. Klusmeyer (eds), *Citizenship Today: Global Perspectives and Practices*. Washington, DC: Carnegie Endowment for International Peace, pp. 278–315.

Laden, A. and Owen, D. (eds) (2007) *Multiculturalism and Political Theory*. Cambridge: Cambridge University Press.

Lægaard, S. (2016) Contextualism in normative political theory, in W.R. Thompson (ed.), *Oxford Research Encyclopedia of Politics*. Oxford: Oxford University Press. Available at: https://doi.org/10.1093/acrefore/9780190228637.013.87.

Landry, C. (2012) *The Creative City: A Toolkit for Urban Innovators*. Hoboken, NJ: Taylor & Francis.

Lashta, E., Berdahl, L. and Walker, R. (2016) Interpersonal contact and attitudes towards indigenous peoples in Canada's Prairie cities, *Ethnic and Racial Studies*, 39(7): 1242–60.

Laurence, J. (2011) The effect of ethnic diversity and community disadvantage on social cohesion: A multi-level analysis of social capital and interethnic relations in UK communities, *European Sociological Review*, 27(1): 70–89.

Leconte, C. (2015) From pathology to mainstream phenomenon: Reviewing the Euroscepticism debate in research and theory, *International Political Science Review*, 36(3): 250–63.

Lentin, A. (2014) Post-race, post politics: The paradoxical rise of culture after multiculturalism, *Ethnic and Racial Studies*, 37(8): 1268–85.

Letki, N. (2008) Does diversity erode social cohesion? Social capital and race in british neighbourhoods, *Political Studies*, 56(1): 99–126.

Levrau, F. and Loobuyck, P. (2013) Should interculturalism replace multiculturalism?, *Ethical Perspectives*, 20(4): 605–30.

Levy, J.T. (2000) *The Multiculturalism of Fear*. Oxford: Oxford University Press.

Lewis, R. (2014) The "Death" of state multiculturalism: Examining political discourse in Post-2010 Europe, in R. Blake and N. Walthrust-Jones (eds), *Identities and Borders: Interculturalism, the Construction of Identity*. Oxford: Inter-Disciplinary Press, pp. 3–19.

Ley, D. (2005) *Post-Multiculturalism?*, Research on Immigration and Integration in the Metropolis, Working Paper Series No. 05–18.

Lofland, L.H. (1998) *The Public Realm*. New York: Aldine de Gruyter.

Loukaitou-Sideris, A. (1995) Urban form and social context: Cultural differentiation in the uses of urban parks, *Journal of Planning Education and Research*, 14(2): 89–102.

Low, S.M., Taplin, D. and Scheld, S. (2006) *Rethinking Urban Parks: Public Space and Cultural Diversity*. Austin, TX: Texas University Press.

Lu, J.G., Wang, D.J., Galinsky, A.D., Hafenbrack, A.C., Eastwick, P.W. and Maddux, W.W. (2017) "Going Out" of the box: Close intercultural friendships and romantic relationships spark creativity, workplace innovation, and entrepreneurship, *Journal of Applied Psychology*, 102(7): 1091–108.

Ludwineck, A. (2015) European intercultural mindset: What can the attitudes and perceptions of europeans on intercultural dialogue, integration and discrimination tell the local policymakers, in R. Zapata-Barrero (ed.), *Interculturalism in Cities: Concept, Policy and Implementation*. Cheltenham: Edward-Elgar Publishing, pp. 97–114.

Lüken-Klaßen, D. and Heckmann, F. (2010) *Intercultural Policies in European Cities*. Report, European network of cities for local integration policies for migrants (CLIP). Dublin: Eurofound.

Lutz, H. (2015) Intersectionality: Assembling and dissambling the roads, in S. Vertovec (ed.), *Routledge International Handbook of Diversity Studies*. Abingdon: Routledge, pp. 363–70.

Madanipour, A. (1996) *Design of Urban Space: An Inquiry into a Socio-spatial Process*. Chichester: Wiley.

Madanipour, A. (ed.) (2010) *Whose Public Space? International Case Studies in Urban Design and Development*. London: Routledge.

Mansouri, F. and Ebanda de B'beri, B. (eds) (2014) *Global Perspectives on the Politics of Multiculturalism in the 21st Century: A Case Study Analysis*, Abingdon: Taylor & Francis, pp. 230–40.

Mansouri, F. and Lobo, M. (eds) (2011) *Migration, Citizenship, and Intercultural Relations: Looking Through the Lens of Social Inclusion*. Aldershot: Ashgate.

Martiniello, M. (2001) Towards a post-ethnic Europe, *Patterns of Prejudice*, 35(1): 59–68.

Matejskova, T. and Antonsich, M. (eds) (2015) *Governing through Diversity: Migration Societies in the Post-multiculturalist Age*. Basingstoke: Palgrave Macmillan.

Meer, N. and Modood, T. (2012) How does interculturalism contrast with multiculturalism?, *Journal of Intercultural Studies*, 33(2): 175–96.

Meer, N., Modood, T. and Zapata-Barrero, R. (2016) A plural century: Situating interculturalism and multiculturalism, in N. Meer, T. Modood and R. Zapata-Barrero (eds), *Multiculturalism and Interculturalism: Debating the Dividing Lines*. Edinburgh: Edinburgh University Press, pp. 1–26.

Meer, N., Mouritsen, P., Faas, D. and de Witte, N. (2015) Examining "Post-multicultural" and Civic Turns in the Netherlands, Britain, Germany, and Denmark, *American Behavioural Scientist*, 59(6): 702–26.

Michalowski, I. (2011) Required to assimilate? The content of citizenship tests in five countries, *Citizenship Studies*, 15(6–7): 749–68.

Migration Policy Group (2017) How the intercultural integration approach leads to a better quality of life in diverse cities, Report Council of Europe, Intercultural Cities, written by A.-L. Joki and A. Wolffhardt with the support of T. Huddleston. Summary: Available at: https://rm.coe.int/intercultural-to-the-core-how-the-intercultural-cities-index-can-be-be/168076631b

Miller, D. (2008) Immigrants, nations, and citizenship, *Journal of Political Philosophy* 16(4): 371–90.

Mitchell, D. (2003) *The Right to the City: Social Justice and Fight for Public Space*. New York: The Guilford Press.

Modood, T. (2007) *Multiculturalism: A Civic Idea*. Cambridge: Polity Press.

Modood, T. (2016) Multiculturalism, interculturalisms and the majority, in N. Meer, T. Modood and R. Zapata-Barrero (eds), *Multiculturalism and Interculturalism: Debating the Dividing Lines*. Edinburgh: Edinburgh University Press, pp. 246–65.

Modood, T., Triandafyllidou, A. and Zapata-Barrero, R. (eds) (2006) *Multiculturalism, Muslims and Citizenship: A European Approach*. London: Routledge.

Mouritsen, P. (2008) Political responses to cultural conflict: Reflections on the Ambiguities of the Civic Turn, in P. Mouritsen and K.E. Jørgensen (eds), *Constituting Communities: Political Solutions to Cultural Conflict*. Basingstoke: Palgrave Macmillan, pp. 1–30.

Mouritsen, P. (2012) Beyond post-national citizenship: Access, consequence, conditionality, in A. Triandafyllidou, T. Modood and N. Meer (eds), *European Multiculturalism(s): Cultural, Religious and Ethnic Challenges*. Edinburgh: Edinburgh University Press, pp. 88–115.

Mouritsen, P. (2013) The resilience of citizenship traditions: Civic integration in Germany, Great Britain and Denmark, *Ethnicities*, 13(1): 86–109.

Mügge, L. (2016) Transnationalism as a research paradigm and its relevance for integration, in B. Garcés-Mascareñas and R. Penninx (eds), *Integration Processes and Policies in Europe: Contexts, Levels and Actors* (IMISCOE Research Series). London: Springer, pp. 109–25.

Müller, U., Wagner, A. and Kunz, P. (2011) *Correlation Study between the Intercultural City Index and Other Data: A Study for the Council of Europe*. Bakbasel Economic Research and Consultancy. Available at: https://rm.coe.int/CoERMPublicCommonSearchServices/DisplayDCTMContent?documentId=0900001680495197

Murphy, M. (2012) *Multiculturalism: A Critical Introduction*. London and New York: Routledge.

Musterd, S. and Murie, A. (eds) (2010) *Making Competitive Cities*. Chichester: Wiley.

Nasser, N. (2015) *Bridging Cultures: The Guide to Social Innovation in Cosmopolitan Cities*. Markham, Ontario: 10-10-10 Publishing.

Neal, S., Bennett, K., Jones, H., Cochrane, A. and Mohan, G. (2015) Multiculture and public parks: Researching super-diversity and attachment in public green space, *Population, Space and Place*, 21(5): 463–75.

OECD (Organisation for Economic Co-operation and Development) (2011) *Perspectives on Global Development 2012: Social Cohesion in a Shifting World*. Paris: OECD Publishing.

Page, S.E. (2007) *The Difference: How the Power of Diversity Creates Better Groups, Firms, Schools and Societies*. Princeton, NJ: Princeton University Press.

Parekh, B. (2000) *Rethinking Multiculturalism: Cultural Diversity and Political Theory*. Basingstoke: Palgrave Macmillan.

Passerin d'Entreves, M. (2018) 'Hannah Arendt', in E.N. Zalta (ed.), *The Stanford Encyclopedia of Philosophy*. Available at: https://plato.stanford.edu/archives/win2018/entries/arendt/

Petermann, S. and Schönwälder, K. (2014) Immigration and social interaction, *European Societies*, 16(4): 500–21.

Peters, K. (2011) *Living Together in Multi-ethnic Neighbourhoods: The Meaning of Public Spaces for Issues of Social Integration*. Gelderland: Wageningen Academic.

Peters, M. and Besley, T. (2012) Education, dialogue and interculturalism: New directions and contexts, *Educational Philosophy and Theory*, 44(9): 909–12.

Peters, K., Elands, B. and Buijs, A. (2010) Social interaction in urban parks: Stimulating social cohesion?, *Urban Forestry and Urban Greening*, 9(2): 93–100.

Pettigrew, T.F. (1998) Intergroup contact theory, *Annual Review of Psychology*, 49: 65–85.
Pettigrew, T.F. and Tropp, L.R. (2006) A meta-analytic test of intergroup contact theory, *Journal of Personality and Social Psychology*, 90(5): 751–83.
Pettigrew, T.F. and Tropp, L.R. (2008) How does intergroup contact reduce prejudice? Meta-analytic tests of three mediators, *European Journal of Social Psychology*, 38(6): 922–34.
Pettigrew, T.F. and Tropp, L.R. (2013) *When Groups Meet: The Dynamics of Intergroup Contact*. London: Taylor & Francis.
Phillips, A. (2007) *Multiculturalism without Culture*. Princeton, NJ: Princeton University Press.
Pinxten, R. and Cornelis, M. (2002) What Interculturalism could bring a solution to racism?, in Evens Foundation (ed.), *Europe's New Racism: Causes, Manifestations, and Solutions*. New York and Oxford: Berghahn Books, pp. 211–32.
Pinxten, R., Cornelis, M. and Rubinstein, R. (2007) European identity: Diversity in union, *International Journal of Public Administration*, 30(6/7): 687–98.
Portes, A. and Fernández-Kelly, P. (eds) (2015) *The State and the Grassroots: Immigrant Transnational Organizations in Four Continents*. New York: Berghahn Books.
Portes, A. and Vickstrom, E. (2011) Diversity, social capital, and cohesion, *Annual Review of Sociology*, 37: 461–79.
Putnam, R. (2007) E Pluribus Unum: Diversity and community in the twenty-first century, *Scandinavian Political Studies Journal*, 30(2): 137–74.
Ram, M. and Jones, T. (2008) Ethnic minority business in the UK: A review of research and policy developments, *Environment and Planning C: Government and Policy*, 26(2): 352–74.
Ramarajan, L. (2014) Past, present and future research on multiple identities: Toward an intrapersonal network approach, *The Academy of Management Annals*, 8(1): 589–659.
Rath, J. (ed.) (2007) *Tourism, Ethnic Diversity and the City*. New York: Routledge.
Recchi, E. (2012) *Transnational Practices and European Identity: Theoretical foundations, research developments and policy implications*, paper presented at The Development of European Identity/Identities: Policy and Research Issues conference, European Commission, Brussels, 9 February.
Reynolds, K. (2017) 13 benefits and challenges of cultural diversity in the workplace. [Blog] *Hult*. Available at: www.hult.edu/blog/benefits-challenges-cultural-diversity-workplace/
Richter, A.W., West, M.A., Van Dick, R. and Dawson, J.F. (2006) 'Boundary spanners' identification, intergroup contact, and effective intergroup relations, *Academy of Management Journal*, 49(6): 1252–69.
Risse, T. (2002) Nationalism and collective identities: Europe versus the nation-state?, in P. Heywood, E. Jones and M. Rhodes (eds), *Developments in West European Politics*. New York: Palgrave Macmillan, pp. 72–93.
Risse, T. (2004) European institutions and identity change: What have we learned?, in R.K. Herrmann, T. Risse and M.B. Brewer (eds) *Transnational Identities: Becoming European in the EU*. Lanham, MD: Rowman & Littlefield, pp. 247–72.
Robins, K. and Aksoy, A. (2016) *Transnationalism, Migration and the Challenge to Europe*. London: Routledge.

Roccas, S. and Brewer, M.B. (2002) Social identity complexity, *Personality and Social Psychology Review*, 6(2): 88–106

Roeder, A. (2011) Does mobility matter for attitudes to Europe? A multi-level analysis of immigrants attitudes to European Unification, *Political Studies*, 5(2): 458–71.

Rogers, R. (2008) *Cities For A Small Planet*. New York: Basic Books.

Rother, N. and Nebe, T.M. (2009) More mobile, more European? Free movement and EU identity, in A. Favell and E. Recchi (eds), *Pioneers of European Integration: Citizenship and Mobility in the EU*. Cheltenham: Edward Elgar, pp. 120–55.

Russell, A. (2015) Introduction. In *The Politics of Public Space in Republican Rome*. Cambridge: Cambridge University Press, pp. 1–24

Samovar, L.A., Porter, R.E., McDaniel, E.R. and Sexton Roy, C. (2015) *Intercultural Communication: A Reader*. Boston, MA: Cengage Learning.

Sandercock, L. (2003) Planning in the Ethno-culturally diverse city: A comment, *Planning Theory and Practice*, 4(3): 319–23.

Sandercock, L. (2004) Reconsidering multiculturalism: Towards an intercultural project, in P. Wood (ed.), *Intercultural City Reader*, London: Comedia, pp. 16–21.

Sarmento, C. (2014) Interculturalism, multiculturalism, and intercultural studies: Questioning definitions and repositioning strategies, *Intercultural Pragmatics*, 11(4): 603–18.

Schlenker-Fischer, A. (2010) *Unity in diversity? European and national identities in respect to cultural diversity*. Faculty of Humanities and Social Sciences Institute of Political Science, Working Paper Series 5, Glocal Governance and Democracy.

Schnapper, D. (1998) *Community of Citizens: On the Modern Idea of Nationality*. New Brunswick, NJ: Transaction Publishers.

Schneekloth, L.H. and Shibley, G. (1995) *Placemaking: The Art and Practice of Building Communities*. New York: John Wiley and Sons.

Scholten, P. (2011) *Framing Immigrant Integration: Dutch Research-policy Dialogues in Comparative Perspective*. Amsterdam: Amsterdam University Press.

Scholten, P. and Van Breugel, I. (eds) (2017) *Mainstreaming Integration Governance: New Trends in Migrant Integration Policies in Europe*. Basingstoke: Palgrave Macmillan.

Scholten, P., Collett, E. and Petrovic, M. (2016) Mainstreaming migrant integration? A critical analysis of a new trend in integration governance, *International Review of Administrative Sciences*, 83(2): 283–302.

Schönwälder, K., Petermann, S., Hüttermann, J., Vertovec, S., Hewstone, M., Stolle, D., Schmid, K. and Schmitt, T. (2016) *Diversity and Contact: Immigration and Social Interaction in German Cities*. London: Palgrave Macmillan.

Schuck, P.H. (2006) *Diversity in America: Keeping Government at a Safe Distance*. Cambridge, MA: Belknap Press of Harvard University Press.

Sen, A. (2006) *Identity and Violence: The Illusion of Destiny, Issues of Our Time*. New York: W.W. Norton & Company.

Sen, A. (2010) Equality of what?, in S. MacMurrin and M. Sterling, *The Tanner Lectures on Human Values*, 4 (2nd edn). Cambridge: Cambridge University Press, pp. 195–201.

Sennett, R. (2012) *Together: The Rituals, Pleasures and Politics of Cooperation*. London: Yale University Press.

Shaw, S. (2007) Ethnic quarters in the cosmopolitan-creative city, in G. Richards and J. Wilson (eds), *Tourism, Creativity and Development*. London: Routledge, pp. 189–200.

Simmel, G. (1950) The metropolis and mental life, in K.H. Wolff and G. Simmel (eds), *The Sociology of Georg Simmel*. New York: The Free Press, pp. 409–24.

Simmel, G. (2009[1908]) *Sociology: Inquiries into the Construction of Social Forms*. Leiden/Boston: Brill.

Sklar, A. (1999) Contested collectives: The struggle to define the "we" in the 1995 Québec referendum, *Southern Communication Journal*, 64(2): 106–22.

Solano-Campos, A. (2016) Models of diversity in the Americas: Avenues for Dialogue and Cross-Pollination, in N. Meer, T. Modood and R. Zapata-Barrero (eds), *Multiculturalism and Interculturalism: Debating the Dividing Lines*. Edinburgh: Edinburgh University Press, 178–200.

Solano-Campos, A.T. (2013) Bringing Latin America's "Interculturalidad" into the conversation, *Journal of Intercultural Studies*, 34(5): 620–30.

Staiger, U. (2009) New agendas? Culture and citizenship in EU policy, *International Journal of Cultural Policy*, 15(1): 1–16.

Stevenson, N. (2003) *Culture and Citizenship: Cosmopolitan Questions*. Maidenhead: Open University Press.

Stolle, D., Soroka, S. and Johnston, R. (2008) When does diversity Erode trust? Neighborhood diversity, interpersonal trust and the mediating effect of social interactions, *Political Studies*, 56(1): 57–75.

Syrett, S. and Sepulveda, L. (2011) Realising the diversity dividend: Population diversity and Urban Economic Development, *Environment and Planning A*, 43(2): 487–504.

Sze, F. and Powell, D. (eds) (2004) *Interculturalism: Exploring Critical Issues*. Oxford: Inter-disciplinary Press.

Tadmor, C.T., Galinsky, A.D. and Maddux, W.W. (2012) Getting the most out of living Abroad: Biculturalism and integrative complexity as key drivers of creative and professional success, *Journal of Personality and Social Psychology*, 103(3): 520–42.

Taras, R. (2012) *Challenging Multiculturalism: European Models of Diversity*. Edinburgh: Edinburgh University Press.

Taylor, C. (2012) Interculturalism or multiculturalism?, *Philosophy & Social Criticism* 38(4–5): 413–42.

Teney, C., Hanquinet, L. and Bürkin, K. (2016) Feeling European: An exploration of ethnic disparities among immigrants, *Journal of Ethnic and Migration Studies*, 42: 2182–204.

Titley, G. (2012) After the failed experiment: Intercultural learning in a multicultural crisis, in O. Yael and H. Otten (eds), *Where Do You Stand? Intercultural Learning and Political Education in Contemporary Europe*. Wiesbaden: VS Verlag, pp. 161–180.

Triandafyllidou, A. and Gropas, R. (2015) *What is Europe?* London: Palgrave Macmillan.

Triandafyllidou, A., Modood, T. and Meer, N. (eds) (2011) *European Multiculturalisms*. Edinburgh: Edinburgh University Press.

Tubino, F. and Sinnigen, J.H. (2013) Intercultural practices in Latin American Nation States, *Journal of Intercultural Studies*, 34(5): 604–19.

Tupas, R. (2014) Intercultural education in everyday practice, *Intercultural Education*, 25(4): 243–54.
UNESCO (2009) *Investing in Cultural Diversity and Intercultural Dialogue*. Paris: UNESCO.
UNESCO (2018) *Inclusion through Access to Public Space*. Available at: https://unesco.org/new/en/social-and-human-sciences/themes/urban-development/migrants-inclusion-in-cities/good-practices/inclusion-through-access-to-public-space/
United Nations (2015) *World Urbanization Prospects: The 2014 Revision*. New York: United Nations.
Valentine, G. (2015) Theorizing Multiculturalism and Diversity: The Implications of Intersectionality, in T. Matejskova and M. Antonsich (eds), *Governing through Diversity: Migration Societies in Post-multiculturalist Times*. London: Palgrave Macmillan, pp. 145–60.
Valentine, G., Piekut, A., Winiarska, A., Harris, C. and Jackson, L. (2015) Mapping the meaning of "difference" in Europe: A social topography of prejudice, *Ethnicities*, 15(4): 568–85.
Vertovec, S. (2007) Super-diversity and its implications, *Ethnic and Racial Studies*, 30(6): 1024–54.
Vertovec, S. (2010) Towards Post-multiculturalism? Changing communities, conditions and contexts of diversity, *International Social Science Journal*, 61(199): 83–95.
Vertovec, S. (ed.) (2014) *Migration and Diversity*. Cheltenham: Edward Elgar.
Vertovec, S. (ed.) (2015) *Routledge International Handbook of Diversity Studies*. New York: Routledge.
Vertovec, S. and Cohen, R. (eds) (2002) *Conceiving Cosmopolitanism: Theory, Context and Practice*. Oxford: Oxford University Press.
Vertovec, S. and Wessendorf, S. (eds) (2010) *Backlash against Multiculturalism in Europe: Public Discourse, Policies and Practices*. London: Routledge.
Vidmar-Horvat, K. (2012) The Predicament of intercultural dialogue: Reconsidering the politics of culture and identity in the EU, *Cultural Sociology*, 6(1): 27–44.
Vormann, B. (2015) Urban diversity: Disentangling the cultural from the economic case, *New Diversities*, 17(2): 119–29.
Wagner, A. (2015) Measuring intercultural policies: The example of the intercultural cities index, in R. Zapata-Barrero (ed.), *Interculturalism in Cities: Concept, Policy and Implementation*. Cheltenham: Edward Elgar, pp. 115–35.
Walzer, M. (1986) Pleasures and costs of urbanity, *Dissent*, 33: 470–75.
Warf, B. and Arias, S. (2008) *The Spatial Turn: Interdisciplinary Perspectives*. London: Routledge.
Watson, S. (2006) *City Publics: The (Dis)enchantments of Urban Encounters*. London: Routledge.
Weber, M. (1968) *Economy and Society*. New York: Bedminster Presss.
Weber, M. (1978) *Economy and society: An outline of interpretive sociology*. Berkeley: University of California Press.
Williams, R. (1976) Culture, in R. Williams, *Keywords: A Vocabulary of Culture and Society*. New York: Oxford University Press, pp. 87–93.

Wimmer, A. and Glick Schiller, N. (2003) Methodological nationalism, the social sciences, and the study of migration: An essay in historical epistemology, *International Migration Review*, 37(3): 576–610.

Wise, A. and Velayutham, S. (eds) (2009) *Everyday Multiculturalism*. Basingstoke: Palgrave Macmillan.

Wood, P. (2004) *The Intercultural City Reader*. Stroud: Comedia.

Wood, P. (2015) Meet me on the corner? Shaping the conditions for cross-cultural interaction in urban public space, in R. Zapata-Barrero (ed.), *Intercultura-lism in Cities: Concept, Policy and Implementation*. Cheltenham: Edward Elgar, pp. 53–75.

Wood, P. and Landry, C. (2008) *The Intercultural City: Planning for Diversity Advantage*. London: Earthscan.

Yazbeck Haddad, Y. and Fischbach, R. (2015) Interfaith dialogue in Lebanon: Between a power balancing act and theological encounters, *Islam and Christian–Muslim Relations*, 26(4): 423–42.

Ye, J. (2017) Contours of urban diversity and coexistence, *Geography Compass*, 11(9): 1–8.

Yılmaz, F. (2012) Right-wing hegemony and immigration: How the populist far-right achieved hegemony through the immigration debate in Europe, *Current Sociology*, 60(3): 368–81.

Young, I.M. (1990) *Justice and the Politics of Difference*. Princeton, NJ: Princeton University Press.

Zachary, P. (2003) *The Diversity Advantage: Multicultural Identity in the New World Economy*. Boulder, CO: Westview.

Zapata-Barrero, R. (ed.) (2009) *Citizenship Policies in the Age of Diversity: Europe at the Crossroads*. Barcelona: Cidob Edicions.

Zapata-Barrero, R. (2011) *Anti-immigration Populism: Can Local Intercultural Policies Close the Space?*, Discussion Paper. London: Policy Network.

Zapata-Barrero, R. (2013) *Diversity Management in Spain*. Manchester: Manchester University Press.

Zapata-Barrero, R. (2014) The limits to shaping diversity as public culture: Permanent festivities in Barcelona, *Cities: The international Journal of Urban Policy and Planning*, 37: 66–72.

Zapata-Barrero, R. (2015a) Conclusions: Three building blocks for taking interculturalism seriously, in R. Zapata-Barrero (ed.), *Interculturalism in Cities: Concept, Policy and Implementation*. Cheltenham: Edward Elgar, pp. 185–96.

Zapata-Barrero, R. (2015b) Interculturalism: Main hypothesis, theories and strands, in R. Zapata-Barrero (ed.), *Interculturalism in Cities: Concept, Policy and Implementation*. Cheltenham: Edward Elgar, pp. 3–19.

Zapata-Barrero, R. (ed.) (2015c) *Interculturalism in Cities: Concept, Policy and Implementation*. Cheltenham: Edward Elgar Publishing.

Zapata-Barrero, R. (2016a) Exploring the contours of a EU in-mobility theory: An opportunity-based approach to EU citizenship and the need of a EU "culture of mobility", *Revista Española de Ciencia Política*, 41: 13–38.

Zapata-Barrero, R. (2016b) Theorising intercultural citizenship, in N. Meer, T. Modood and R. Zapata-Barrero (eds), *Multiculturalism and Interculturalism: Debating the Dividing Lines*. Edinburgh: Edinburgh University Press, pp. 53–76.

Zapata-Barrero, R. (2016c) Exploring the foundations of the intercultural policy paradigm: a comprehensive approach, *Identities: Global Studies in Culture and Power*, 23(2): 155–173.

Zapata-Barrero, R. (2016d) Diversity and cultural policy: Cultural citizenship as a tool for inclusion, *International Journal of Cultural Policy*, 22(4): 534–52.

Zapata-Barrero, R. (2017a) Interculturalism in the post-multicultural debate: A defence, *Comparative Migration Studies*, 5(14): 1–23.

Zapata-Barrero, R. (2017b) Mainstreaming and interculturalism's elective affinities, in P. Scholten and I. Van Breugel (eds), *Mainstreaming Integration Governance: New Trends in Migrant Integration Policies in Europe*. Basingstoke: Palgrave Macmillan, pp. 191–213.

Zapata-Barrero, R. (2017c) Multi-level intercultural governance in Barcelona: Mainstreaming comprehensive approach, in Special Issue edited by R. Zapata-Barrero, T. Caponio and P. Scholten, 'Symposium on theorizing "The Local Turn" in the governance of immigrant policies: A multilevel approach', *International Review of Administrative Sciences (IRAS)* 83(2): 247–66.

Zapata-Barrero, R. (2017d) The intercultural turn in Europe: Process of policy paradigm change and formation, in F. Mansouri (ed.), *The Promise and Challenge of Intercultural Dialogue: From Theory to Policy and Practice*. Paris: UNESCO Publishers, pp. 169–93.

Zapata-Barrero, R. (2018a) Rejoinder: Multiculturalism and interculturalism: Alongside but separate, *Comparative Migration Studies*, 6(20): 1–12.

Zapata-Barrero, R. (2018b) Transnationalism and interculturalism: Overlapping affinities, in J.E. Fossum, R. Kastoryano and B. Siim (eds), *Diversity and Contestations over Nationalism in Europe and Canada*. London: Palgrave Macmillan, pp. 89–122.

Zapata-Barrero, R. and Rezaei, S. (eds) (2019) Diaspora governance and transnational entrepreneurship: The rise of an emerging social global pattern in migration studies, Special Issue, *Journal of Ethnic and Migration Studies*. DOI: 10.1080/1369183X.2018.1559990

Zapata-Barrero, R. and Triandafyllidou, A. (eds) (2012) *Addressing Tolerance and Diversity Discourses in Europe: A Comparative Overview of 16 European Countries*. Barcelona: Fundació Cidob.

Zapata-Barrero, R., Caponio, T. and Scholten, P. (2017) Introduction: Theorizing the "Local Turn" in a multilevel governance framework of analysis. A case study in immigrant policies, in Special Issue edited by R. Zapata-Barrero, T. Caponio and P. Scholten, 'Symposium on Theorizing "The Local Turn" in the Governance of Immigrant Policies: A multilevel approach', *International Review of Administrative Sciences (IRAS)* 83(2): 241–6.

Zapata-Barrero, R., Dähnke, I. and Markard, L. (eds) (2018) *Immigrant Incorporation in Political Parties: Exploring the Diversity Gap*. London: Routledge.

Zuma, B. (2014) Contact theory and the concept of prejudice: Metaphysical and moral explorations and an epistemological question, *Theory and Psychology*, 24(1): 40–57.

INDEX

action theory, 71
administrations, 3, 17, 26, 31, 75
   civic, 24
   public, 109
anti immigrant, 4, 8, 17
anti-immigration, 9, 34, 108
antiracism, 102, 106
assimilation, 6, 36
assimilationism, 28
assimilationist, 47
authority, xiii, 20, 26, 28, 77, 81
autonomy, 42, 44, 89, 97

benefits, xiv, 101–3, 105
   competitive, 101
   economic, 103–4
   potential, 103
   private, 100
   social, xii, 100, 102, 114
Bouchard, 18, 20, 30, 79, 82, 86
Bouchard-Taylor report, 20
boundless multiculturalism, 9, 27

Canada, 19–21
Canadian multicultural policy, 20
Cantle, 29–31, 79, 83, 111
Cantle Report, 5
cities, 15–18, 24–28, 86–87, 94–96,
    100–102, 109
   creative, 105
   diverse, 94, 105
   diversity-dividend, 101
   heterogeneous, 95
   home, 57
   large, 113
   main, 59
   modern, 49
   wealthier, 109

citizens, xiii, 13, 15–16, 22, 92, 102
   community of, 80, 91
   fellow, 89
   majority-national, 15, 47
   minority-ethnic, 15
   native-born, 110
   passive, 91
   urban, 28
citizenship, xi–xii, 17, 21, 25–26, 31, 89–93
   behavior, 92
   civic-national, 82
   communitarian, 91
   cultural, 78, 96, 106
   focus, xi
   national, 35, 83
   national-civic, xiii, 14
   regimes, 32
   republican, 28, 93
   studies, xiii, 26, 28, 90–91
   tests, 9, 11, 31, 118, 127
   union, 39
   urban, 26
Citizenship Traditions, 90–92
city, 16–18, 23–24, 28–29, 52–53,
    94–96, 109
   framework, 23
   functions, 24
   -government, 17
   hall, 77
   identities, 47; *see also* identities
   level, 16, 18, 28, 52
   life, 98
   -network strategy, 24
   planners, xii
   project, 28
   realms, 53
   tensions, 5
   turn, 26

INDEX

civic
  integration, 9
  nationalists, 14, 29
  turn, 10–11
cohesion, xi–xii, 76, 80, 83, 109–11
  promotion, 110
cohesion strands, 80–81, 83–86
common interest, 56, 64, 72
communication, 14, 56, 67, 83, 96, 105
  non-verbal, 69
  professional, 104
  vertical, 79
communitarian, 90, 92
Communitarianism, 91
communities, 30–31, 33, 41–42, 57, 59, 91
  adoptive, 96
  cohesive, 83
  local, 57, 93
  migrant, 3
  minority, 5
  national, 32, 47, 59
  political, 41
  segregated, 9
  single, 57
  social, 59
community centre, 92
community cohesion, 8, 30, 59, 79, 83, 111
community gardens, 88, 92, 96
community halls, 74
community interrelations, 91
community-building, xi, 28, 57
competitive advantage of cities, 102
complexity, 48, 115
  diverse, 46
  social identity, 56–57
conflict, 27, 30, 33, 56, 69, 110
  diversity-related, 27, 69, 97, 114
  ethno-religious territorial, 19
  political, 34
  unprecedented, 34
  zones, 79
consensus, 18, 112
  general, 40
  scholarly, 105
constructivist, 38, 44, 76, 80–81, 84–86

contact, 11–16, 54–56, 63–67, 69–74, 82–85, 94–96
  equal status, 64
  eye, 108
  internal personal, 55
  interpersonal, 5, 66
  managed, 65
  reduced, 13
  situational, 66
contact promotion, xii, 43, 70, 74, 77, 85
contact theory, 63–64, 66, 70
  social-psychology's, 38
contact zones, 14, 31, 52, 69
contact-promotion, 86
contacts-based approach, 12, 14, 16
context, 4–5, 19–21, 46, 53–54, 66, 82–87
  conflictive, 71
  current, 51
  determinate, 46
  epistemological, 11
  global, 25
  new, 3, 8, 10, 54
  super-diversity, 15
  supportive, 96
context of diversity, 17, 79
contextual approach, 71
contextual factors, 7–8, 51
contractual strand, 80–86
conviviality, 97–99
cosmopolitan, 3, 41, 48, 57–58, 85, 128
  community, 58
  culture, 58
  identity, 43
  mindset, 59
  position, 58
  problem, 58
  strand, 29
  vision, 44
cosmopolitanism, xiv, 26, 49–50, 57–59, 116
Council of Europe (CoE), 17, 22–23, 25–26, 29, 84, 101
creativity, xii, 27, 78, 80, 84–86, 103
crisis, 4, 32, 41–42
  current identity, 33
  economic, 27

financial, 3, 17
ideological, 51
life-threatening, 34
ontological, xiv, 33
ontological European identity, 34
unprecedented, 33
cultural capital, 11, 78, 93, 103
cultural diversity, 31, 42–43, 72, 95, 104–5, 112–13

democracy, xii, 22, 95, 108, 110–11
development, 10–11, 78–80, 84, 86, 88, 112–13
  aesthetic, 78
  cultural, 79
  mutual, 84
  personal, 78
  rapid, 113
  social, 84, 86
dialogue, 20, 24, 67, 69, 71, 111
  inter-faith, 23
  international, xiv
  intrapersonal, 55
dialogue promotion, 25
diversity advantage, 29–30, 80, 101, 103–4
diversity-contacts, 64, 66–68, 70–71, 80, 85, 88–89
  inter-personal, 69
  potential, 78
  promotion, 76, 79, 89, 101, 112
  zone, 92
diversity-recognition, xi, 34, 42–43, 58, 66, 106

epistemology, 50, 116
equality, xi–xii, 5–6, 14, 42, 64, 84
  principle of, xi, 5, 8
equality conditions, 74
equality of rights, 28, 42
ethnicity, 11–12, 34, 48, 88, 91, 107
Europe, 8–9, 11, 13, 20–22, 24–25, 111–12
  migrants as pioneers of, 38
  post-ethnic, 44
European cities, 52, 109
European identity, xiv, 22, 33–34, 37–45, 116
  -building process, 33

formation, 33, 36, 38, 41–42, 44
largest, 37
markers of, 4–5, 36
studies, 40
Euro-scepticisms, 34, 36

freedom, 25, 35, 37, 42, 44

governance, 7, 17, 31, 34, 53, 77
groupism, 12, 48
groups, 7, 28, 30, 34, 37, 110
  distinct, 94
  ethnic, 12, 22, 48, 53
  explicit, 17
  heterogeneous, 84
  minority, 64
  particular national, 47
  privileged cultural-differentiated, 107

homogeneous societies, 109, 114
human rights, xi–xii, 9–10, 42, 58, 108, 110–11
humanity, common, 16, 30, 63–64

ICC *see* Intercultural Cities
ICD *see* Intercultural Dialogue
identities, 5–6, 40, 42–44, 46, 56, 58–59
  complex, 48, 54, 107
  cultural, 6, 22
  inclusion, 39, 43–44, 88, 93, 95–96, 101
  inequalities, xii, 5, 31, 33, 113, 115
  social, 74, 77–78, 83
  innovation, 78, 80–81, 84–86, 102, 104–5, 114
intercultural, 28, 31, 55, 76–77, 92–94, 106
intercultural approach, 20, 105, 109
Intercultural Cities (ICC), 17, 24, 26–27, 53, 121, 127
intercultural citizenship
  approach, xiii, 17, 27, 70–71, 74, 99
  debates, xiii, 76, 115
  paradigm, 3–5, 12–14, 16–17, 19, 30–31, 71
  practices, 88, 95
  republican, 92, 94, 97

intercultural contact, 39, 44, 70, 74, 83, 103
Intercultural Dialogue (ICD), 21–26, 71
interpersonal cultural development, 79
intersectionality, 70, 109

Kymlicka, xiv, 8–9, 47, 59, 114

Landry, 29–30, 80, 105

mainstreaming, 17, 51–52
   approach, 53
   policies, 3, 48, 50–53
majority/minority nexus, 50, 81–82, 115
migration, 4, 19, 23, 25, 112, 115–16
migration studies, xiii, 15, 27, 50, 57
Modood, 14, 21, 30
multicultural citizenship, xiii, 14, 17–18, 27, 30, 47
   approach, 27, 48, 51
   paradigm, 4, 6–10, 12, 15–16, 27, 29–30
multiple identities, xi, 3, 43, 47–48, 56
mutual understanding, 13, 22, 25, 27, 83

national citizens, xiii, 13, 15, 40, 46, 54
   see also citizens
national community, 91
national identities, 10, 36–38, 53, 55–56, 79–82, 90–91; see also identities
national tradition, xiii, 77, 79; see also tradition
national-civic citizenship paradigms, 10–11, 14–15, 17
nationalism, 12, 48
nationality, 3, 43, 48, 55, 91, 107–8
naturalization policies, 13, 45

participation, xi–xii, 23, 25, 28, 55, 72
policy paradigms, 14, 17–18, 20, 27, 50, 53
   emerging intercultural citizenship, 18
power relations, 8, 15, 20, 33, 37, 74
   asymmetrical, 31
   unbalanced, 69, 113, 115

public benefits, 101–2, 105–6, 111
public good, 112
public spaces, 27–28, 67, 69–70, 73–74, 87–99, 106–7
   shared, 101, 111, 113–14

Quebec, 19–20, 77, 82; see also Canada

racism, 4, 30, 47, 58, 102, 106–8
religions, 6–7, 22, 34, 38, 47–48, 63–64
republican tradition, 89–93, 95
republicanism, 87, 89, 92–93

security, xiii, 23, 34–35, 59, 105, 107
shared spaces, 74, 80, 83, 87, 99, 106
social capital, 8, 13, 16, 77, 83, 109–11
social cohesion, 5, 26–28, 83, 106, 109–10, 114
social conflicts, 79–80, 83, 85–86, 114
social ties, 56, 106–7
socialization, xiii, 16, 36, 96, 106
spatial experience, 93, 99
stereotypes, xiii, 64, 66, 98, 107–8, 113
strangers, 57, 67–69, 94, 98
super-diversity, xii, 7, 15, 47, 49–50, 85
supremacists, xiii, 4, 108, 116

togetherness, 96, 98, 113
tolerance, 8, 23, 44, 56, 65, 95
tradition, 38, 47, 79–82, 85–86, 89, 91
transnational nationalism, 55
transnationalism, xiv, 48–50, 54, 57, 116
trust, 15, 31, 59, 96, 103, 109–11

Unesco, 88, 110
unity and diversity, 20, 79, 81

Vertovec, 10, 58

Wood and Landry, 29–30, 80

xenophobia, 17, 26, 34, 102, 106–8, 113
xenophobic narratives, 47, 108–9